TWAYNE'S WORLD AUTHORS SERIES

A Survey of the World's Literature

RUSSIA

Charles Moser
The George Washington University

EDITOR

Nikolay Leskov

TWAS 523

Drawing by I. E. Repin, 1889

N. S. Leskov

NIKOLAY LESKOV

By K. A. LANTZ
University of Toronto

TWAYNE PUBLISHERS
A DIVISION OF G. K. HALL & CO., BOSTON

Copyright © 1979 by G. K. Hall & Co.

Published in 1979 by Twayne Publishers,
A Division of G. K. Hall & Co.
All Rights Reserved

Printed on permanent/durable acid-free paper and bound
in the United States of America

First Printing

Library of Congress Cataloging in Publication Data

Lantz, K. A.
Nikolay Leskov.

(Twaynes' world authors series ; TWAS 523 : Russia)
Bibliography: p. 161–63
Includes index.
1. Leskov, Nikolay Semenovich, 1831–1895—
Criticism and interpretation.
PG3337.L5Z7495   891.7'3'3   78-14757
ISBN 0-8057-6364-3

Contents

About the Author

Kenneth Lantz is Assistant Professor of Russian at Erindale College, University of Toronto. He received his M.A. and Ph.D. from the University of Toronto. His publications on Russian literature have appeared in the *Slavic and East European Journal* and *Studies in Short Fiction*.

Preface

The writings of Nikolay Leskov (1831-1895) are much less known to Western readers than are those of his contemporaries. This relative but quite undeserved obscurity is partly due to his language: his stylistic brilliance inevitably fades in translation. Partly it is due to his subject matter, so firmly grounded in the Russian reality of his day that it may be less readily appreciated by non-Russian readers. Partly it is due to the unjust and brutal treatment he was accorded by contemporary critics, who gave him a reputation so unsavory that he was neglected for many years after his death. But mostly it is due to the fact that Leskov does not have one or two "central" works — specifically, novels — which would conveniently express his manner and his major concerns. His contemporaries — Tolstoy, Dostoevsky, Turgenev — each have one or two major novels which, having read, a reader can say with some justification that he "knows" the writer. But Leskov has no novels strong enough to secure a major reputation. Although he was a prolific writer, his works so differ in manner and in content that one searches in vain for any one or two which would best sum him up. The result is that those who have read Leskov at all usually know only a few of his writings, which are necessarily unrepresentative.

This study is intended to sketch a literary profile of Leskov for the general reader and to provide a brief reference work for the specialist. To do this means to outline in brief his literary career and provide at least a minimum of background for his works. It also means discussing as many of his writings as possible, including some which may be only moderately successful yet highly revealing. A profile, after all, must indicate both the peaks and the hollows. Shorter works must be grouped into coherent patterns. Leskov himself collected stories in cycles, but was not entirely consistent in his choices; so that his word need not necessarily be taken as final. I have arranged his writings for discussion generally on thematic lines, except for his novels and chronicles. Space limitations preclude much detailed analysis, but in choosing between lengthy discussion of a few works and a more general study of many, the latter is clearly the course which best provides a profile of a writer such as Leskov.

Space limitations also preclude much discussion of Leskov's style. To be sure, his language is one of the things which have earned him a lasting reputation in Russian literature. But style is a topic for a more specialized work (several are noted in the bibliography) and for a more specialized reader. Leskov's journalism, while undoubtedly of interest, receives little attention here, as do some of his other writings which straddle the boundary between fiction and journalism.

Much of the research was carried out while on a Government of Finland Scholarship and I would like to express my gratitude for this support, as well as to the staff of the Slavic Collection, Helsinki University Library. My thanks are also due to the University of Toronto for a grant-in-aid of research. Finally, I am indebted to the work of many Soviet Leskovists and also to two American scholars, William Edgerton and Hugh McLean, who have done so much to acquaint English-speaking readers with Leskov's writings.

K. A. LANTZ

University of Toronto

Chronology

All dates are "old style," that is, twelve days earlier than the Gregorian calendar.

1831 Born in Gorokhovo, Orel Province, February 4.

1841 Enters Orel *gymnasium*.

1846 Leaves the *gymnasium*; the end of his formal education.

1847 Begins work as clerk in the Orel Criminal Court.

1849 Transfer to Kiev to State Treasury.

1853 Marriage to Olga Smirnova.

1857 Begins work with Scott and Wilkins. Travels extensively in Russia for three years.

1860 Returns to Kiev in May after end of service with Scott and Wilkins; resumes civil service career; resigns in November. First piece of journalism appears in June.

1861 Moves to St. Petersburg in January and works as a full-time journalist; on staff of *Russkaya rech* in Moscow, July–December. Final separation from first wife.

1862 First story ("A Cancelled Affair") appears in March. Article on St. Petersburg fires (May 30) causes storm; leaves Russia in September as correspondent for *Severnaya pchela*; visits Central Europe; spends three months in Paris.

1863 Returns to St. Petersburg in March. In July and August visits Pskov and Riga to study schools for Old Believers.

1864 Publication of *No Way Out* begun in February.

1865 "Lady Macbeth"; second (common-law) marriage to Ekaterina Bubnova.

1866 Birth of son, Andrey. *The Islanders*.

1867 Drama *The Wastrel* performed in St. Petersburg, November 1.

1869 Beginnings of association with M. N. Katkov and *Russky vestnik*.

1872 Publication of *Cathedral Folk* begun in April.

1873 "The Sealed Angel" and "The Enchanted Pilgrim."

1874 Appointed member of "Scholarly Committee," Ministry of

Education. Break with M. N. Katkov.
1875 Second trip abroad (May–August): visits Paris, Marienbad. "At the World's Edge."
1877 Breakup of second marriage.
1878 *Little Things from Bishops' Lives.*
1881 "Lefty."
1883 Dismissal from post in Ministry of Education (February).
1884 Third trip abroad (June–July); while in Marienbad learns that his *Little Things* are included in "dangerous" books removed from public libraries.
1887 "Pamfalon the Clown," "The Sentry"; first meeting with Tolstoy (April).
1888 "Beautiful Aza."
1889 Publication of *Collected Works* begun; volume 6 confiscated (August 14); first attack of *angina pectoris* (August 16).
1890 "The Mountain"; visit to Tolstoy at Yasnaya Polyana (January 24–26).
1891 "Nightowls."
1893 "The Beast Pen."
1894 "A Winter's Day."
1895 "The March Hare." Death on February 21.

CHAPTER 1

Biographical Sketch

I *Early Life*

NIKOLAY Leskov's childhood years introduced him to the diversity of Russian life, a diversity he found even in his own family background. His paternal ancestors had traditionally been clergymen in the village of Leski in Orel Province of South-Central Russia. The writer's father, Semen Dmitrievich, completed his seminary training in 1808 but stubbornly refused to follow the clerical career mapped out for him. Semen Dmitrievich's father was so incensed when he learned that his only son had ended the family tradition that he drove him from the house with only forty kopeks which his mother managed to slip him as he fled. The ex-seminarian found work in Orel as a tutor in the families of local gentry and soon earned a reputation as an honest and capable worker, which led to a post in the Ministry of Finance. After service in the Caucasus, where he quickly rose to acquire the hereditary status of a noble, he returned to Orel and in 1830 married a former pupil, Marya Alfereva.

The picture Nikolay Leskov paints of his father is of a stern, uncompromisingly honest man who distinguished himself as a legal investigator through his talent for uncovering wrongdoing. In 1839 he came into conflict with the local governor and, in keeping with his stubborn character, refused to make the expected apology. He was thus forced to leave the service at the age of fifty with no pension and purchased Panino, a very modest estate of fifty serfs in the Kromy District of Orel Province. The few hundred rubles of yearly income that Panino provided were scarcely enough to support a household that soon grew to include seven children. Semen Leskov himself worked in the fields, but a series of poor harvests, drought, and squabbles with the peasants undermined his health and left him an embittered man. He died of cholera in 1848. Although Nikolay spent relatively little time with his father, there is no doubt that the image of this uncompromising and upright man profoundly influenced his equally uncompromising son.

Leskov's mother's family, the Alferevs, were of the minor nobility and had fled Moscow before Napoleon's invading armies, losing all their possessions in the Moscow fire of 1812. The family resettled in Orel and Leskov's maternal grandfather eventually found a living managing the estate of an eccentric landowner, Mikhail Strakhov. Strakhov, whom Leskov describes as "boorish, despotic and, apparently, slightly mad,"[1] married one of the Alferev daughters, a woman some forty years his junior. It was on Stakhov's estate, Gorokhovo, that Marya Leskova gave birth to her first son, Nikolay, on February 4, 1831. Although his family lived in Orel until 1839, Nikolay spent most of his first eight years on the Gorokhovo estate and received his early education together with his cousins, the Strakhov children.

Leskov's mother managed to cope with the trying conditions of her marriage and to run the household on a sharply restricted budget. After the end of her husband's civil service career she became the virtual head of the family. She was a strong-willed, even domineering woman with a "quick and impatient character"[2] who could spare little love for her firstborn son. Leskov inherited her energy and practicality as well as her impatience and difficult temperament. Several of her relatives also exerted considerable influence on Leskov's life. He often refers to his maternal grandmother, Akilina Alfereva, as a woman of pious simplicity who often took him on pilgrimages to local monasteries. His maternal uncle Sergey became a Professor of Medicine at Kiev University and did much to help with Leskov's later education. His aunt Alexandra married a Russianized Englishman named Scott, who played a large role in Leskov's later career.

Leskov's family background thus exposed him to the principal social classes of his day: both grandmothers were of merchant stock; his mother was of the gentry; his paternal grandfather of the clergy; and his father a civil servant. His life at Panino gave him firsthand knowledge of Russia's largest class, the peasants. "In the country," he says, "I lived in complete freedom which I enjoyed as I wished. My playmates were peasant children with whom I lived in complete harmony and understanding. I knew the way of life of the

common people down to the finest details and understood to the
finest nuances how the people from the master's house treated
them..." (11. 12). Leskov also mentions his nurse, a coachman,
and a miller as sources of folk tales and popular lore which captured his imagination.

Religion — though of an unconventional variety — played its
part in Leskov's early years. He himself said, "I had religious
feeling from childhood, and of a fortunate kind, that is, the kind
which from an early age began to reconcile faith with reason" (11.
11). He describes his mother's beliefs as strictly conventional and
largely formalistic; he was more impressed by his father's insis-
tently independent approach to religion. Semen Leskov rarely attended church and did not observe any of the rites apart from Confession and Holy Communion. Leskov also had some acquaintance
with the numerous Old Believers (Orthodox schismatics) and other
sectarians who lived in the Gostomlya[3] area and speaks of his
early sympathy for them.

Leskov's formal education proceeded no more smoothly than
had his father's career in the civil service. The Strakhovs' tutors
educated him along with his cousins; but here, as so often in his
later life, he was cast in the role of the outsider who did not fit readily into the group. His aptitude made the comparative slowness of
his classmates all the more evident and soon earned him the hostility of the Strakhovs. Leskov's grandmother Alfereva finally asked
his father to bring the child back to Panino, where he spent two
happy years free from studies. In 1841 the ten-year-old Leskov was
sent to Orel to board with a midwife so he could attend the local
gymnasium. His few remarks about this period of his life paint a
bleak picture of an overcrowded, stifling classroom staffed by ill-
qualified or indifferent teachers who relied on the birch rod to hold
the attention of their pupils. In an autobiographical fragment he relates how a drunken teacher once cut off the ear of a pupil with a
ruler.[4] In the autumn of 1846 Leskov left the school after completing only three classes. He himself never gave any precise
reasons for this sudden end to his formal education, but when one
considers the conditions in the school, the lack of parental supervi-
sion, his own prickly, independent nature, and the example of his
father's departure from the seminary, it seems scarcely surprising.
His informal education, of course, had begun much earlier and
continued throughout his life. He was an avid reader from childhood and prided himself on his erudition. But the lack of any offi-

cial diploma remained a sore spot throughout his life: his son recalls how annoyed and embarrassed Leskov would become when
asked in all innocence which university he had attended.

Leskov obtained a post in the Orel Criminal Court in 1847 and in
slightly more than a year had advanced to assistant department
head. The firsthand acquaintance he here acquired with dramatic
legal cases served him well as material for both journalism and
fiction. But life in the sleepy provincial capital could not fully satisfy a talented and ambitious young man. In December 1849 his
uncle Sergey Alferev helped him arrange a transfer to Kiev, where
he obtained a post as assistant to the head clerk in the recruiting
section of the State Treasury. In 1852, at age twenty-one, he was assigned to the ardous and often heartbreaking task of organizing the
annual levy of recruits for the army. His work here left strong impressions: the sight of fourteen-year-old Jewish boys being sent for
military service after being declared of age by hired perjurers, for
example, was the basis for "Vladychnyi sud" (Episcopal Justice,
1877).

Leskov's experiences in Kiev also helped shape his creative
personality. These were, in effect, his university years, and although he received no diploma, he did broaden his horizons im-
mensely as he discovered new areas of culture. Living with his
uncle, Leskov became acquainted with most of the young profes-
sors at Kiev University and attended some lectures. Through his
good friend Stepan Gromeka, special assistant to the governor-
general of Kiev, Leskov was introduced to the city's literary set and
took part in amateur theatricals. The city itself provided a constant
source of stimulation with its splendid heritage of ancient churches
richly decorated with medieval frescoes and icons. This direct link
to an older tradition stimulated Leskov's already keen interest in
iconography and antiquities of all sorts. But the city was more than
a museum of past culture; its present was a cosmopolitan blend of
Ukrainian, Polish, and Russian elements. Leskov mastered both
Polish and Ukrainian and immersed himself in both cultures.
Kiev's linguistic diversity helped sharpen his ear for the nuances of
language. His debt to Polish literature in particular is an area that
remains to be investigated.[5]

The Kiev years also gave Leskov his first family. In April 1853 he
married rather suddenly — and, as it developed, unwisely — Olga
Vasilevna Smirnova, the daughter of a Kiev merchant. She was a
woman of little beauty or intelligence and emotionally unstable in

the bargain. It seems probable that Leskov's motives were primarily mercenary: he was, after all, talented and eager to make a career for himself, but with no means of his own, while her father was a man of considerable wealth. The marriage lasted eight years (there seems little doubt that it would have ended earlier had Leskov not been away from home through 1857–60) and produced two children: Dmitry, who died in infancy, and Vera, born in 1856. When Leskov returned to Kiev in 1860 he found life with Olga intolerable, and when he obtained work as a journalist in St. Petersburg he welcomed the opportunity to leave his wife. Olga's mental condition deteriorated in later years, and from 1878 until her death in 1909 she was confined to an asylum in St. Petersburg. To Leskov's credit, he visited her regularly and helped support her financially.[6]

Leskov achieved some success in the civil service and in 1856 was promoted to the rank of provincial secretary, twelfth of the fourteen ranks in the hierarchy. But selecting recruits was difficult and unpleasant work which failed to satisfy his essentially artistic temperament. Russia's defeat in the Crimean War, which revealed all the shortcomings of the regime of Nicholas I, coupled with the excitement of rapid economic growth in the early years of Alexander's reign, led many civil servants to seek work with newly established private businesses. Thus in May 1857, Leskov took leave of absence to work with the firm of Scott and Wilkins.

Alexander Scott, Leskov's maternal uncle, was a Russianized Englishman whose father had settled in Russia early in the nineteenth century and had organized a firm which, among its other activities, managed the extensive estates of the very prominent Naryshkin and Perovsky families. Both father and son were enterprising and energetic and worked actively, if not always successfully, to introduce new methods of agriculture into Russia. The younger Scott's personality made a lasting impression on Leskov and provided material for several stories. Scott's sense of personal dignity, his sense of justice, and his critical, "foreign" attitude toward Russian life gave Leskov a living example of the strong-willed independence which emerges as one of the prime values in his fiction. Scott's firm was based in Penza Province, but Leskov's work led him to many obscure corners of the Russian Empire, "from the Black Sea to the White and from Brody to Krasny Yar" (10. 311). The firm's activities were widely varied ("We plowed the land, planted sugar beets and were preparing to make sugar and distil spirits, saw timber, split barrel staves, make saltpeter and cut

parquet flooring . . . [6. 8]), but Leskov himself was most often involved in supervising the resettlement of peasants. Peasants were
forcibly torn away from their native villages and moved by barge,
the cheapest form of transportation, to new estates being opened
up in the South and East. Scenes of the breakup of families and of
the inhumane conditions of transport left deep impressions on
Leskov and gave him insights into the peasant mentality that he uti-
lized in journalism and fiction. Yet there were also less gloomy
scenes — comical adventures, encounters with colorful people —
that supplied him with a stock of raw material he was to draw on
for the rest of his career. In later years he looked back on this
period as the happiest of his life.

The firm of Scott and Wilkins prospered for a time but soon encountered financial difficulties, and Wilkins, the more solvent partner, withdrew, leaving Scott to pick up the pieces and Leskov to find
other employment. He returned to his civil service post in Kiev but
resigned after seven months.[7] It was clear that he had talents
beyond those of an administrator. The letters in which he had so
vividly described his travels while working for Scott had attracted
the attention of friends who encouraged him to take his writing
more seriously. Even while working for Scott, he had spent some
time in St. Petersburg where his Kievan acquaintances had helped
him make contacts with journalistic circles. A colleague of
Leskov's uncle, Professor A. P. Valter, invited Leskov to contribute to a weekly medical journal, *Sovremennaya meditsina*
(Contemporary Medicine). Leskov was also recommended to the
Countess Salias de Tournemire as a suitable correspondent for her
newly established liberal newspaper, *Russkaya rech* (Russian
Speech). It was in this capacity that the thirty-year-old Leskov arrived in St. Petersburg in January 1861.

II   *Leskov's Journalism in the Sixties*[8]

Russian society was transformed in the 1860s. The defeat in the
Crimea in 1856 had made plain to everyone, including the new tsar,
the urgent need for modernization of the country. The fact that
Alexander II was known to be disposed to reform opened the
floodgates for new ideas and marked the beginning of a new era in
Russian intellectual history. Nikolay Shelgunov, a radical journalist active in the sixties, describes this new atmosphere in his
memoirs: "As soon as the Crimean War had ended and everyone

caught a breath of the new, freer air, everything that had any intellect in Russia, from the very highest levels to the lowest, began to think as it has never thought before. Sevastopol caused people to think and it awoke in everyone a critical attitude which became common property.... Everyone began to think and to think with one tendency, the tendency of freedom, of creating better conditions of life for each and all.''[9] This new critical spirit, coupled with an easing of the censorship regulations, promoted a sudden expansion in Russian journalism. Periodicals sprang up filled with passionate articles exposing the shortcomings of the existing order and earnestly discussing proposals for reform.

Leskov plunged into this ferment of ideas with a series of articles in 1860–61 on a wide range of topics fully in tune with the spirit of the times. His first published article exposed the profiteering of a Kiev bookseller who was selling copies of the Gospels at twice the indicated price.[10] In another he dealt with the unglamorous but very practical topic of the lack of proper toilet facilities in public buildings.[11] Still other articles pointed out the difficulties young people faced when seeking careers in business; described the lamentable state of housing for workers in Russian cities; campaigned for the eradication of drunkenness (while another article lamented the lack of taverns where one could drink cheaply and comfortably).[12] His "A Few Words About Doctors in Recruiting Offices" detailed the shocking abuses in the system of recruitment and the widespread bribery of doctors who certified recruits.[13] "A Few Words About Police Physicians in Russia" accused provincial doctors in broadside fashion of living on bribes and provoked the first of the long series of journalistic tempests which were to mark each stage of Leskov's career.[14]

The first real boost for Leskov's career as a journalist came in the spring of 1861, when he published a series of articles and reviews in the respectable "thick" journal, *Otechestvennye zapiski* (Notes of the Fatherland). Here too he relies on his commercial experience with Scott and Wilkins: for example, a lengthy and well-documented article, the first Leskov wrote but did not immediately publish, dealt in detail with vodka-distilling in Penza Province. Although the tone of these articles is still rather strident, the underlying philosophy is that of a liberal champion of *laissez-faire* who has great faith in education, reforms, and enlightened economic progress. But on the whole the articles of the first two years reveal not only a young man sincerely angered by the abuses he exposes, but also a novice journalist eager to make his mark as a crusader. He writes in a militant, polemical style using heavy doses of sarcasm. His basic position is firmly grounded in his own experience and he does not, as did so many of his contemporaries, abandon common sense in favor of purely theoretical impulses. Even here, however, Leskov the artist coexists with Leskov the journalist: he enlivens his articles with anecdotes, bits of dialogue, and colorful words and expressions.

In the summer of 1861 Leskov moved to Moscow to work with the editor of *Russkaya rech,* Evgeny Feoktistov. All went well until his estranged wife arrived unexpectedly and set off another squabble with his journalistic colleagues. The Countess Salias de Tournemire and her friends the Novosiltsev sisters (whom Leskov was later to pillory in his novel *Nekuda* [No Way Out]) took his wife's part, and after a number of stormy scenes Leskov broke with the countess and returned to St. Petersburg at the end of 1861, full of bitterness.

By this time the period of harmony within the intelligentsia was over as their initial all but unanimous support for the reforms gave way. Disenchantment with the actual Act of Emancipation of the serfs, an increase in peasant disturbances, and unrest among the students tended to polarize opinion among the intellectuals. Leskov later remarked: "Soon after this [the Emancipation of 1861] a great schism occurred in literature: out of one camp, with one common tendency toward good, there developed two parties, the 'gradualists' and 'the impatient ones'. . . . I remained then with the gradualists, whose moderation appeared to me to be more sound."[15] Journals became much more conscious of party lines and the polemical heat generated in the following years scorched more than a few. Mikhail Katkov and Nikolay Strakhov both published attacks on the radicals and Leskov followed suit, deploring in shrill tones the rigidity and dogmatism of the other party:

The well-known freedom of opinion, for which civilized mankind has always struggled, and its equally well-known manifestation in Russian journalism, so joyfully welcomed by the public, has now almost ceased to exist. . . . There are no longer any discussions about opinions, nor are there any carefully worked out opinions; one-sided opinions have appeared, pronounced like infallible judgments for which the author, in the event of the slightest disagreement with him, will launch a *personal* attack upon his opponent. . . . The senseless shouts of these buffoons, who have

studied the people by means of literary anthologies, are disgraceful....
They behave in the literary world like peasants at their meetings — everyone shouts and no one listens.[16]

To be sure, Leskov's own frenzied shouts made a sizable contribu-
tion to the journalistic din of the sixties. Yet his complaints — the
decline of civilized debate, the tendency toward party-line dogmatism, the turn to personal attack when rational argument failed —
were very real ones. He himself was to suffer from them more than
any other writer of his day.

Leskov now began to turn away from his earlier economic journalism and to publish in other organs of the "gradualists." Articles
and fiction appeared in Dostoevsky's *Vremya* (Time) and *Epokha*
(Epoch), and in the spring of 1862 he joined the staff of *Severnaya
pchela* (Northern Bee). Although the newspaper hewed to a moderate liberal line, it still had an unsavory reputation from the time
when its founder, Faddey Bulgarin, had collaborated with the
police of Nicholas 1 to help oppress Pushkin.

It was in *Severnaya pchela* that Leskov published his first short
stories of peasant life, and here too that he achieved his first notoriety. A literary feud had erupted between the radicals grouped
around the journal *Sovremennik* (The Contemporary) and the
moderates, of whom *Severnaya pchela* was a minor but vocal representative. At the same time, the political situation had grown very
tense with an increase in student and peasant disturbances and a
series of revolutionary proclamations circulating about the streets.
In late May of 1862 a series of fires broke out in St. Petersburg. On
the twenty-eighth a large fire burned the central shopping district of
the city, destroying several hundred wooden shops, private homes,
and some government buildings. There was little doubt in the
minds of the populace that the fires were due to arson and it took
scant imagination to link them with the upsurge in revolutionary
activity of the past year. The fact that the last large fire was but one
of a series added to the sense of panic and helplessness in the face
of a mysterious group of terrorists and arsonists plotting to destroy
the city.[17] The apparent inability of the authorities to stop the destruction intensified that sense of helplessness. A contemporary expressed the mood in a diary entry: "The city is obviously in danger.
We have, thank God, sufficient troops. But would it not be appropriate to set up stronger patrols and even to cordon off the more
dangerous and suspicious areas? But there is nothing of the sort.

With such weakness on the part of the government one can, of course, expect even greater disasters."[18] Students, as one of the more visibly radical elements in society, found themselves not only under suspicion but in some instances in physical danger from attack by mobs. Leskov himself managed to save one student from assault by a group of enraged citizens. It was under these circumstances that he wrote a fateful editorial in *Severnaya pchela*. He began by describing the rumors or arsonists at work in the city and by pointing out the potential danger from mob action to "the type of people to whom the arsonists supposedly belong." "As to how well founded are the suspicions of the people," he continued, "and how appropriate are their fears that the fires are connected with the recent abominable and seditious proclamations calling for the destruction of the whole civil order of our society, we do not venture to judge. . . . But however that might be, even if the St. Petersburg fires should really have something in common with the senseless escapades of political demagogues, still they do not in the least appear to us to be dangerous for Russia if the St. Petersburg authorities do not fail to take account of all the means they can dispose of at the present moment." He concluded with an unequivocal request that the authorities make public any information they had regarding the origin of the fires and carry out a full investigation: "Is there any basis at all for the rumors now circulating in the capital about the fires and incendiaries? Diabolical scoundrels must not be spared, but neither should we endanger a single hair of a single head that lives in the capital and is exposed to the censure of a terrified population which may not be without danger."[19]

This might all appear to be reasonable enough to an observer removed from the immediate emotions of the scene by more than a hundred years, but the reaction it caused arose more from the immediate feelings of party strife than from cool common sense. The article was read as an attack on the student movement; Leskov was visited by a deputation from the young generation which accused him of setting the government against the students; he received anonymous threatening letters; and, perhaps the most serious consequence, he acquired a reputation as "the scourge of the radicals" and even, in some quarters, as a police spy. This reputation was to poison his relations with a large part of the literary world for the next twenty years. "Leskov's personal torments," his son says, "were immeasurable. They 'lodged in his liver' for the rest of his life. He positively trembled at their every mention. It was a constantly bleeding wound which would not heal. And it was all the more painful because he stubbornly considered it to be undeserved."[2]

In June 1862 Leskov fled from the tempest in the capital for a visit to his mother in Orel Province and in September left for Europe as a correspondent for *Severnaya pchela*. His itinerary led him through Lithuania, Belorussia, the Western Ukraine, Poland, and Bohemia (in present-day Czechoslovakia), and finally to Paris in December. En route he dispatched a lively and vivid series of articles[21] which testify to his continued interest in practical economics and technology as well as to his growing tendency to "fictionalize" his journalism. His reports on trade, railways, and the development of cities are enlivened by extensive dialogue, details of local color, and descriptions of interesting people he encountered. One article even creates a small drama based on fragments of a conversation overheard from an adjacent hotel room, a technique he was to put to good use later in "Polunoshchniki" (Nightowls). In Paris Leskov, always determined to be at the center of things, took up residence in the Latin Quarter. His Paris dispatches show little knowledge of or interest in the French intellectual life around him; his associations were mainly with the Slavic communities of Paris and his accounts of his stay are full of sarcasm toward the manners of the Russian community. He continued his literary work — "Ovtsebyk" (The Musk-ox) was written here — and on the whole led a busy, carefree life which helped him recover from the strains of the previous spring.

III *Leskov and the Nihilists*

Leskov returned from Paris in March 1863 to find a changed mood in Russia. The fires of the previous year, the social unrest, and particularly the Polish rebellion of 1863 had driven many liberals, formerly intoxicated by the heady atmosphere of the previous few years, into the camp of the conservatives. A reviewer writing in January 1863 noted sardonically: "St. Petersburg seems to have grown calmer and faded. After the May fires many people hastened to launder their inner accoutrements — their ideas, convictions, and other fine-sounding things, especially where for some reason they feared that they might smell of smoke. The color ran from the cheap material."[22] The polarization in literary circles was complete, and Leskov lost the contacts he had once had among the leftists. He began working in *Biblioteka dlya chteniya* (Reading Library), a journal of moderate liberal views, and published in it his articles on the Russian colony in Paris, a long tale, "Zhitie odnoi baby" (The Life of a Peasant Woman), and his novel *No Way Out*. His return from Paris marks the beginning of a new stage in his career; henceforth he would first be a writer of fiction and only second a journalist.

Aside from purely literary work, however, Leskov was commissioned by the Minister of Education, Alexander Golovnin, to study the possibility of separate schools for the children of Old Believers. Such schools had existed in some areas thirty years earlier but had been closed by the authorities. Rather than have their children educated under the influence of the official church, the parents allowed them to grow up illiterate. Leskov traveled to Pskov and Riga in the summer of 1863 and through his knowledge of their situation and his experience in dealing with people managed to win their confidence. His study[23] recommended establishment of separate schools, but the Ministry, faced with opposition toward granting additional rights to sectarians, did not act on Leskov's proposals. His experience with Old Believers did, however, provide material for several stories and pieces of journalism.

Shortly after Leskov's return from Paris there appeared in the pages of *Sovremennik* Nikolay Chernyshevsky's novel *Chto delat'?* *(What is to be Done?)*. It caused a sensation and was immediately taken up as a bible for practical action by the young and radical. Leskov's response to it not only provides us with a statement of his own beliefs at the time, but also illuminates many pages of his own writings.[24] Surprisingly, he has some warm words to say about Chernyshevsky and even about his novel, although only on the basis of his own rather peculiar reading of it. He begins by dismissing the novel as a work of art as "beneath any criticism; it is simply ridiculous." But he insists that the novel is useful since it does answer the question posed by its title. The glaring inconsistency in Leskov's argument (although the novel is artistically worthless, its characters are convincing and, apparently, models for emulation) leads one to suspect that his real motivation is not to praise Chernyshevsky's achievement. Leskov's interpretation of Chernyshevsky makes the latter appear as a moderate liberal proposing the same sort of gradual development and reform that Leskov saw as the answer to "what is to be done?" Thus Leskov turns an apparent tribute to the most renowned radical of the day into an oblique attack on the radicals as a whole: by arguing that Chernyshevsky's ideas were not really revolutionary he hoped to cut the ground from beneath the feet of those who were promoting revolution in Chernyshevsky's name.[25] Leskov expresses admiration for Chernyshevsky's characters because they are independent, original, and men and women of action. In so doing he is able to fire off salvos at the pseudo-nihilists for their lack of originality and for their impracticality. If Chernyshevsky's scheme seems utopian, Leskov argues, it is only because there are too few good people available to realize it. Leskov thus quite approves of nihilism in the sense in which he defines it — as a healthy skepticism and independence of belief coupled with the capacity for positive action to build a better society. Chernyshevsky's revolutionary bias becomes only a matter of ethics, of individual rather than social regeneration.

Leskov spent most of 1863 writing a novel which, in part at least, was a response to *What is to be Done?* and which he intended as a summing up of the age in which he lived. It also created a sensation and profoundly influenced the remainder of his career. The first chapters appeared in January 1864 and passed quietly enough since they dealt with life in the provinces and touched upon the radical movement only obliquely. Later books attracted the attention of the censors, who were being doubly cautious after the appearance of Chernyshevsky's novel. The heads of both the Censorship Committee and the Third Section (Secret Police) examined the book. Leskov wrote some years later that "the censor never suppressed any other book with such frenzy as *No Way Out.* . . . I lost my head and cursed the hour in which I got the idea of writing this ill-fated work."[26]

The censor's mutilation did not diminish the furor the novel caused. Issues of *Biblioteka dlya chteniya* were quickly sold out and a separate edition, published shortly after the last installment in the journal, was gone in three months. The public at large was fascinated by what purported to be an inside view of the much-discussed nihilist movement. Radical critics, and most liberal ones as well, were infuriated by Leskov's vicious caricatures of well-known figures in Moscow and St. Petersburg intellectual circles. "In essence it is simply some poorly overheard gossip carried over into literature," fumed one radical critic.[27] Leskov did nothing to calm the situation when he published an "Explanation" insisting with much vehemence and little conviction that his characters bore no resemblance to living persons. The most serious attack came from

Dmitry Pisarev, the uncompromising critic and leading theoretician of the nihilist movement, who pronounced what was scarcely less than a literary death sentence on Leskov: "I am very interested in the following two questions: 1) Is there now, apart from *Russky vestnik* (Russian Herald), even one journal that would dare to print on its pages anything issuing from the pen of Mr. Stebnitsky [The nom de plume under which Leskov published most of his early fiction] and signed with his name? 2) Is there in Russia even one honorable writer who would be so rash and indifferent to his reputation that he would agree to contribute to a journal which adorns itself with the tales and novels of Mr. Stebnitsky?"[28]

No Way Out made Leskov a pariah to much of the literary world. He recalls that people would leave the room when he entered. When Mavriky Volf, publisher of a later edition of the novel, mentioned that he had received letters threatening to burn his shop, Leskov countered that he himself had received more than a dozen letters threatening to shoot or to hang him. Even years later he could not speak of the affair without bitterness. He wrote in an unpublished articles:

For twenty years running ... I bore vile slander and it spoiled but a little — *just one life*.... For a number of years I was even deprived of the possibility of working.... And all this on account of one novel, *No Way Out*, where I simply drew a picture of the development of the struggle of socialist ideas with the ideas of the old system. There were neither lies nor tendentious fabrications in the novel but simply a *photographic reproduction* of what occurred. The most sympathetic figure in the novel is even a *socialist* (Rayner, whom I drew from Arthur Benni). Now Prince Bismarck says that we must in some way come to terms with the socialists, but in my novel I showed with a living character that socialist ideas have some good in them and can be adapted to a system which is desirable for the greatest possible good for the greatest possible number of people. In the literary world, however, it was decided that this novel was "written on the orders of the Third Section, which had paid me a lot of money for it." This ruined my position in literature and since, apart from literature, I had no other activities, it *ruined my life for an entire twenty years*. There was no possibility of casting off this vile slander because people *only talked* and did not write about it ... They limited themselves to hints in print. ... They wrote things about me such as "This is not bad, but *it smells like a denunciation*."[29]

The bitterness with which these lines were written twenty years after the fact is remarkable. Even discounting Leskov's tendency to self-pity and exaggeration (his novel was by no means as innocent as he implies; he was not totally deprived of work, although he was barred from many publications), the cloud which he conjured up in *No Way Out* did hang over his head for many years.

IV   *Second Family and Literary Successes*

Leskov once again fled from the storms of St. Petersburg and spent the last half of 1864 and the beginning of 1865 in the calmer waters of Kiev. Here he met Ekaterina Bubnova, an intelligent and cultured young woman who was separated from her husband. Her firm character and practicality attracted Leskov and seemed to promise another chance for a happy family life. Since both she and Leskov were already legally married, they were forced to live common-law. He returned to St. Petersburg with her and her four children and settled in a comfortable flat overlooking the Tauride Gardens. Here in July of 1866 his son and future biographer Andrey was born. Family life was reasonably happy, and Leskov soon gathered a large circle of acquaintances from the more conservative elements of St. Petersburg literary circles. A few years of comparative calm ensued during which he produced some of his finest writings. But finances became a problem: he now had six dependents and few markets for his work.

The journals which had previously accepted his writings closed or changed hands: *Severnaya pchela,* where he had really begun his full-time journalism, closed in 1864; Dostoevsky's *Epokha*, which had published his "Lady Macbeth," closed in 1865 as did *Biblioteka dlya chteniya.* Leskov had published some of his finest works of the sixties in *Otechestvennye zapiski,* but its editor and Leskov's good friend Stepan Dudyshkin died unexpectedly in 1866, leaving the journal in the hands of Andrey Kraevsky, who was not on good terms with Leskov. He turned to the conservative *Literaturnaya biblioteka* (Literary Library) until it, too, closed in 1868. Leskov's financial position grew so precarious that he was forced to write an emotional appeal for a loan to the Literary Fund, an organization set up to help writers in need, only to face the humiliation of a refusal when none of its committee members would agree to act as guarantor. He turned once again to journalism, writing regular articles and feuilletons for the dailies *Birzhevye vedomosti* (Stock-Exchange News) and *Russky mir* (Russian World). Between 1869 and 1871 he published more than a hundred articles here, commenting on happenings in Russia, particularly on church matters and education, as well as drama criticism and book reviews, again chiefly of religious and historical works.[30] Considering the volume and the need for haste, the unevenness of these writings is understandable, but they do show the breadth of his interests and his talent for lively writing.

Leskov's literary stock took a sudden upswing when he began publishing in Katkov's respected and influential *Russky vestnik*, a journal which counted the greatest names in contemporary Russian literature among its contributors. Katkov's journal had become decidedly more conservative in the later sixties and published a series of "anti-nihilist" novels including Leskov's *Na nozhakh* (*At Daggers Drawn*). Katkov also published the two works which won Leskov real fame (rather than notoriety) among Russian readers: *Soboriane*, (Cathedral Folk, 1872) and "Zapechatlennyi angel" (The Sealed Angel, 1873). The latter story attracted the attention of the tsar and tsarina, and their favorable reaction was communicated to Leskov by their Adjutant-General, Sergey Kushelev. "In 1873," remarks his son, "'The Angel' threw open the doors of the most dizzying aristocratic salons to him."[31] Kushelev became a good friend and did much to ease Leskov's financial problems. Through Kushelev's influence Leskov in 1874 was appointed a member of the special "Scholarly Committee" of the Ministry of Education at a salary of 1,000 rubles per year. The post was no sinecure, but the work, involving selection of books for school and public libraries, was compatible. For the next nine years Leskov attended the regular Tuesday meetings of the committee and soon established himself as an authority on church matters and history. His firsthand knowledge of the peasants made him a good judge of what would be appropriate reading matter for them. His reviews for the committee also provided the basis for a number of journal articles. The government post, the success of Leskov's writings (collections of stories written in the sixties were published in 1867 and in 1869), and Katkov's generous payments eased his financial burden.

V   *Self-Examination*

The seventies were a period of transition and self-examination for Leskov, a period in which he chose a new and much weightier role for himself as a writer. His literary career, in spite of its ups and downs, seemed firmly established, yet he still felt "that all that I write is not at all what I want to and am able to write . . ." (10. 335). He urged a friend, the historian and editor Peter Shchebalsky, to reread his (Leskov's) writings and compose a critical article about them: "Be as strict as you can with me, but help me to comprehend myself and end my vacillation" (10. 313). Evidence of Leskov's changing views can be seen even in *Cathedral Folk*, which, in spite of its anti-nihilist element, shows a move away from the conventional orthodoxy of most of the conservative camp. The most evident sign of Leskov's changing attitude was his break with Katkov. In May of 1873 Katkov had refused to publish Leskov's "Ocharovannyi strannik" (The Enchanted Pilgrim). Then Katkov's editors made a number of arbitrary changes in the text of Leskov's *Zakhudalyi rod* (*A Family in Decline*), leading him to break off publication in the autumn of 1874. As Leskov said later, "Katkov had great influence on me, but it was he who first said to Voskoboynikov [Katkov's assistant] during the publication of *A Family in Decline*: 'We are mistaken, this man is not one of ours!' We parted (over the view of the aristocracy) and I did not complete the novel. We parted politely but firmly and finally and he said then once more: 'There is nothing to regret — he is certainly not one of ours.' He was right, but I did know *whose* I was" (11. 509).

Katkov's sudden realization that Leskov was not "one of ours" is understandable and has a very real basis. What first appeared in *A Family in Decline* to be an affirmation of the positive role of the aristocracy after the reforms of the sixties, gradually revealed itself as an attack not only on the aristocracy, but on contemporary society as a whole. Indeed, the word *rod* in the title has a far broader meaning than "family," including "kin," "clan," "stock," "genus," thus expressing Leskov's growing pessimism over what he saw as a decline in the moral level of society in general. But the break with Katkov was an extremely painful one and sapped Leskov's will to work. His position was again desperate enough for him to seek employment outside literature, and he enlisted the help of the Slavophile journalist Ivan Aksakov: "To be successful this time and not to fear death from hunger I must go a different way from the one I followed in serving Russian literature and Russian thought as best I could. *Russky vestnik* was the last journal to which I could somehow cling even while suffering there considerable constraint — and now even this is finished. . . . Therefore, so as not to give up literature entirely, I must get away from it for a time and become independent from this overpowering journalism. It is impossible to work in the journals today with the tyranny which exists there and my situation now is the best proof of this" (10. 362). Aksakov recommended Leskov as one experienced in commerce to the industrialist Vasily Kokorev, and Leskov did edit and evaluate a study of the Baku oil industry for him. Kokorev would make no further commitments to employ Leskov full-time and the relationship broke off.

Coupled with these difficulties were marital and family problems. Andrey Leskov's detailed biography of his father reveals little of the relationship between his parents. Leskov rarely wrote to his wife, and those letters which have survived are either written in irritation or concern business matters. But the picture of Leskov-*paterfamilias* which does emerge is one of a domestic tyrant easily provoked to corporal punishment whose lack of patience and highly strung temperament made life difficult for all members of the family. Andrey states that his father cherished the ideal of a happy domesticity (and family life is certainly an ideal in Leskov's fiction), fondly picturing the family gathered around the table in the evening bathed in the soft light of the lamp. "But in real life . . . someone only had to drop a teaspoon, spill jam on the table cloth, or brush against the table leg with his foot to cause the thunder and lightning to break out. The infuriated head of the household would seize his glass of tea and leave the table, its lamp, and all those gathered around it. With an offended air he would retreat to his lonely study which had long been beckoning him. We at the table would all grow animated . . ."[32]

As marital relations became increasingly strained and his literary career drifted further into the doldrums, Leskov decided once more to seek respite in Europe:

I want to go abroad about the 15th of May; I want, even if only temporarily, not to see all of the things which have deprived me of my strength and capacities. I hope to attach myself to some group of French pilgrims and *walk* with them to Lourdes. Perhaps the religious exuberance of these people, whom I know thus far only for their lack of religiosity, wil absorb me and I will not think about those things on which my thoughts are so agonizing and so fruitless. Apart from this I myself do not know why I am going, but the need to go away for the longest possible time is overpowering. (10.397)

He left St. Petersburg on May 9, 1875 and, after stops in Moscow and Kiev, spent the month of June in Paris. But the city had far less appeal for him than it had had thirteen years earlier: the summer was cold and rainy; the planned pilgrimage to Lourdes had to be canceled because of floods on the Garonne; the ceaseless din of the Paris streets tormented his already frayed nerves. Leskov moved from the lively Latin Quarter which had once so entranced him and found quieter accommodation with the Russian scholar Fedor Buslaev. His nervous condition ruled out any serious literary work, and he found little in French life to give him the hoped-for spiritual uplift. But he did find some genuine religious feeling among the Russian Jesuits he associated with in Paris. Aksakov had asked him to seek out Ivan Gagarin, a member of an old princely family who had emigrated to France in 1843 and became a Jesuit. Gagarin had known Pushkin and had been accused of writing the infamous "cuckold letter" which led to Pushkin's death. After meeting Gagarin, Leskov became convinced that these accusations were false and later stated his views in a journal article.[33] Leskov was attracted by the sincere religiosity of the Jesuits he met and impressed by their well-run schools and pedagogical methods which contrasted so markedly with the scant attention the Russian clergy paid to education. Leskov left Paris in July to spend six weeks taking the waters in quiet Marienbad, where the routine of simple, nourishing meals, rest, mud baths, and numerous glasses of mineral water at last soothed his nerves and restored some of his creative forces. He returned to Russia in August via Prague, Dresden, Hamburg, and Warsaw.

The trip finally did bring to a head the process of self-examination and evaluation in which Leskov had been engaged for the previous several years. As he wrote to Shchebalsky in July:

In general I have become a "turncoat" and no longer burn incense to many of my old gods. Above all I have broken with ecclesiasticism, about which I have read to my heart's content in works that are forbidden in Russia.... More than ever I believe in the great significance of the church, but nowhere do I see that spirit which becomes a society bearing the name of Christ. ... I will say only this: had I read all the many things I have now read on this subject and heard all that I have now heard, I would not have written *Cathedral Folk* as I did write it, for that would have been distasteful to me. Instead, I am now itching to write about a Russian heretic — an intelligent, well read, and free-thinking spiritual Christian who has passed through all doubts for the sake of his search for Christian faith and has found it only within his own soul. I would call this story "Fornosov the Heretic" and I would publish it — but where could I publish it? Oh, these "tendencies." (10.411–12)

It would be a mistake to speak of a sudden "conversion" brought about solely by Leskov's readings and theological discussions while abroad. But the respite of a few months in Europe did what he hoped it would do — it enabled him to collect his thoughts and sum up the process of self-examination begun in the early seventies. There is no doubt that Leskov did begin a new course, not only in matters of religion but also in politics and literature. The break with the conservatives of *Russky vestnik* had deeper causes than Katkov's heavy-handed editing of Leskov's writings. In September of 1875, for example, Leskov wrote to Shchebalsky, a man whose conservative views he had previously regarded as close to his own, that "our views have developed differently and this has happened not long ago" (10. 423). Most important was his changed attitude toward his own literary work. He chose a role as moralist and critic of his times, and the didactic and satirical tendencies in his writings grew steadily stronger. Although he was still desperately in need of money, he declined offers to write purely sensational novels so that he could, as he said, "observe, judge, and sum up this dead time in living images" (10. 435). Writing now became a very serious business.

All the strength which he had gathered while abroad was needed on his return home. The winter of 1875–76 was one of the most difficult of his life, and his letters of the period — even when one takes into account the characteristic element of self-dramatization — are written in a tone of utter despair: "I have literally nothing to live on and nothing to put my hand to: I can find work nowhere and have nowhere to gather up strength to work. And I cannot support my family on one thousand rubles. I can expect nothing and will probably go to my brother's in the country to work as a bailiff so as at least not to die of hunger or be thrown into debtor's prison. A situation without *a gleam of hope and my spirit has fallen into despair*, preventing me from thinking and hoping" (10. 426). Leskov could find work only in a few lesser-known publications, and through 1876 and 1877 published stories and articles in religious periodicals, such as *Pravoslavnoe obozrenie* (Orthodox) Review) and *Strannik* (The Wanderer), or in small-circulation newspapers such as *Krugozor* (Horizon) and *Grazhdanin* (The Citizen). Only in November of 1877 did his prospects improve when, again through the efforts of S. E. Kushelev, he was given another government post, this time in the Ministry of State Property. The additional 1,000 ruble salary with relatively few duties eased some of the pressure. His drama *Rastochitel'* (The Wastrel) was revived on provincial stages in the same year, providing both financial and moral support. In 1878 he was invited to write for the influential newspaper *Novosti* (The News) and continued to publish there for the next ten years. In 1879 Aleksey Suvorin asked him to contribute to the large daily *Novoe vremya* (New Times), and he also began writing regularly for *Peterburgskaya gazeta* (St. Petersburg News), a popular newspaper which paid well. Later in the same year he found more work in the newly established *Istoricheskiy vestnik* (Historical Herald), almost the only "thick journal" where he could publish from 1880–85.

But tensions of the previous years had already contributed to the final breakup of Leskov's second marriage. Leskov's prickly temperament alone would have minimized the chances for a happy marriage, but the continual frustrations of his literary work, financial problems, and disputes with his wife over the education of their son (Leskov insisted Andrey follow a military career, his wife wanted a classical education) strained it to the point of rupture. He spent the summer of 1876 apart from his wife at a dacha near Vyborg, and a year later Leskov and his son moved to new quarters, although he continued to see her regularly.

VI   *Critic and Moralist*

Leskov was not alone in his disillusionment with the official church, but his characteristic skepticism and independence made him wary of allying himself with others who were similarly disenchanted with Orthodoxy. One such group centered on the English evangelist Granville Lord Radstock, whose visit to Russia in 1874 had won him a large following among the upper levels of St. Petersburg society. Leskov followed Radstock's progress with the same interest he devoted to all religious phenomena. He was eager to learn more of the movement and became acquainted with one of the leading St. Petersburg Radstockites, Yuliya Zasetskaya. In the summer of 1876, while a guest at her dacha on the Gulf of Finland, he persuaded her of his keen interest in Radstockism; she, believing that anything unfavorable would be kept confidential, told him much about Radstock's personal life and the inner workings of the movement. Leskov's instincts as a journalist, his concern only with painting a colorful portrait of this new messiah, overcame his scruples and he produced a venomous portrait of Radstock and his followers, *Velikosvetskii raskol* (The Schism in High Society).[34] Just as in *No Way Out*, he presents an exposé of one of the most discussed movements of the day. Although he does admit that Radstock has had some beneficial influence on those to whom he had preached, the portrait of him is laden with sarcasm and the evangelist emerges as something of a pious fool, playing at religion in the same way the nihilists of *No Way Out* played at revolution. Leskov's main theological objection to Radstock is the superficiality of his concept of Christianity, which relies solely on the redemptive powers of Christ for salvation. Zasetskaya was shaken by this breach of trust and wrote Leskov a dignified letter reproaching herself for being mistaken in him.

With a ready market for his writings, Leskov was now financially secure; following the separation from his wife, he no longer suffered the strains he found in family life. A few years of stability ensued and his output increased. As he wrote to Suvorin, "In peaceful conditions I can work readily and sometimes even satisfactorily; when there is a disburbance I drop everything at once and cannot continue, Such is my nature, unhappily sensitive and impressionable."[35] Thus between 1881 and 1889 he produced a prodigious amount of journalism as well as an impressive body of fiction. His fictional works tend to be shorter than those of his previous years, and he concentrates on what he does best: the artfully told, intriguing anecdote or "personal recollection." He did not abandon the novel but — chiefly because of censorship problems — none of the three novels he began publishing were finished. From the late seventies he became increasingly caught up in his chosen role as a moralist and critic. Two main trends appear in his later fiction: he produces a series of positive figures — "righteous men" who come from all areas of life and from different historical periods, people whose moral goodness places them at odds with their society. The second trend, the negative, consists of a series of satirical writings in which he attacked the church hierarchy and looked with increasing malice on what he saw as a decaying and frivolous society. As he told his biographer Anatoly Faresov: "My latest writings on Russian society are very severe.... My readers do not like these works because of their cynicism and straightforwardness. But I really do not want to appeal to my readers. Let them choke on my stories, as long as they read them. I know how to appeal to readers, but I no longer want to do so. I want to flog and torment them.''[36]

The comparative calm at this point of his career was disrupted by another of the unsettling incidents which marked his life, his dismissal from his post on the Scholarly Committee in 1883. While Leskov had taken his committee duties seriously, he never hesitated to condemn works which he felt were unsuitable for popular reading, and on a number of occasions had published his opinions. His desire to "flog and torment" readers had emerged in several anticlerical works which found little favor among the ruling circles, whose mood grew increasingly reactionary after the assassination of Alexander II in 1881. In February 1883, he published an account of some little-known eighteenth-century scandals among the Moscow clergy which described how a certain Father Kirill once rode around the altar of his church on the back of another priest and once urinated on the caftan of the verger, who was wearing it at the time. The minister of education informed Leskov that such literary activity was not compatible with his official post in the ministry. Leskov would not resign and refused to allow the customary phrase "voluntary retirement" in the order for his dismissal. "This is how it must be," he told the minister, "if only for the obituaries: for mine and for yours.''[37] Thus ended Leskov's civil service career (he had retired from his other government post in 1880). The whole affair again unsettled Leskov's nerves, so much so that for a time he suffered from hallucinations.

The following summer, on the advice of a doctor, Leskov traveled to Marienbad to take the waters once more. He lost some excess weight and his health improved. He returned in August after brief stops in Prague and Warsaw. While at Marienbad he learned that another of his anticlerical writings, *Melochi arkhiereiskoi zhizni* (Little Things from Bishops' Lives), was among the 125 works ordered removed from public libraries in Russia.

Leskov had for some time wanted to publish his *Collected Works*, that palpable testimony that a writer had firmly established himself. In 1883 he had negotiated with the St. Petersburg publisher Mavriky Volf over such an edition, but Volf died on the day the contract was to be signed. In 1888 he concluded an arrangement with Suvorin for a ten-volume edition. The first five volumes were published in the spring of 1889 and sold reasonably well. In August appeared volume 6, containing "Little Things from Bishops'

Lives" and other anticlerical writings. Although all of these had
previously been published elsewhere, the book was confiscated.
Leskov suffered this further abuse from the censor deeply (the chief
censor was now Evgeny Feoktistov, whom Leskov had caricatured
in *No Way Out*); not only was there helpless anger at the fate of the
book, but also the more immediate financial problem. The contract
with Suvorin stipulated that publishing costs and profit would be
guaranteed. Leskov had accepted 11,000 rubles in advance from
Suvorin, and it now seemed to him that he was facing financial
ruin. Leskov himself insisted that the first symptoms of the *angina
pectoris* from which he suffered in his last years occurred on
August 16, 1889, when he first learned of the confiscation of
volume 6. Eventually, however, some material was freed by the
censor and he was able to substitute other works for those still
banned and so save himself. But the effects of this affair remained
with him for the rest of his life. "I suffered dreadfully over this edition," he wrote to Suvorin. "I began it as a healthy man and with
the sixth volume I got an incurable illness (neuralgia of the chest or
angina pectoris.)"[38]

VII *Leskov and Tolstoy*

Leskov's growing moral concerns in his last years inevitably led
him to the dominant moralist of the age, Tolstoy. He had long been
interested in Tolstoy the artist, and in 1869 had published a series of
articles on *War and Peace* in which he paid tribute to the "enormous talent, intellect and spirit, but also a (thing all the more rare
in our enlightened age) his grand character, worthy of esteem."[39]
Tolstoy's disenchantment with the official church and his turn to
religious and moralistic writings in the 1880s interested Leskov even
more, particularly when Tolstoy's views appeared to be so close to
his own. "What we have is Byzantinism and not Christianity," he
wrote in 1883, "and Tolstoy is engaged in a worthy struggle against
this, wishing to show through the Gospels not so much the 'path to
Heaven' as the *meaning of life*" (11.287). Tolstoy's basic Christianity expressed in active love for one's fellow men was essentially the
same as the ideal that Leskov had attempted to formulate through
positive figures in his stories of the later seventies.

A firmer association between the two writers developed in 1885,
when Vladimir Chertkov[40] invited Leskov to publish a story in the
Posrednik (The Intermediary) series. They began corresponding —

Leskov's letters were considerably lengthier and more effusive than Tolstoy's — and met for the first time in April of 1887. Leskov's letters to Tolstoy are full of pleas for advice and guidance, coupled with apologies for asking for advice. At times he assumes an almost supernatural relationship between him and Tolstoy: he speaks of "communing" (*soobshchenie*) with Tolstoy while reading his works. Leskov's attitude to Tolstoy can only be described as worshipful, and his remarks about him are so extravagant as to be embarrassing: "For me Tolstoy is my sacred shrine on this earth — 'the priest of the living God, clothed in the truth....' He has enlightened me and I am indebted to him more than to the repose of earthly life; the blessing of his astonishing mind has revealed to me the path to life without end, a path on which I was wandering in confusion and from which I would undoubtedly have strayed" (II.536). It is not surprising that Tolstoy, in spite of his interest in Leskov the man ("What an intelligent and original man!" he remarked after their first meeting"[41]) and his admiration for some, but by no means all, of his writings, felt uncomfortable in such a relationship. As he once remarked to an editor of his, Lynbov Gurevich: "Yes, he sometimes writes to me ... Only his tone is somehow ... it is too ... It's unpleasant ... But then you probably know what I mean."[42]

Ultimately, Tolstoy provided support for Leskov by systematizing and clarifying those ideas which he had not fully worked out himself and by providing assurance that he was not totally alone in his views. As he wrote to Tolstoy:

I was myself approaching that which I saw in your teachings, but I was always afraid that I was mistaken because, although the same thing shone in my consciousness as that which I recognized in your teachings, everything was chaos with me — confused and vague, and I did not rely on myself. But when I heard your elucidation, so logical and powerful, I understood it all, just as if I were recollecting, and I no longer needed my own ideas, and I began to live in the light which I saw from you and which was all the more pleasing for me because your light was imcomparably brighter and more powerful than the one in which I fumbled about unaided. (11.519)

In spite of Leskov's worship of Tolstoy, his own temperament scarcely suited him for the role of a Tolstoyan. As a close acquantance remarked:

He openly called himself a disciple of Tolstoy and wanted to bow his head meekly before the genius of the great writer. In questions of social ethics he constantly, persistently, and with that particular quick temper which was characteristic of him in everything, proclaimed himself to be of the same mind as Tolstoy. He wanted to submit to Tolstoy's proscriptions in matters of personal morality as well; he wanted to be a vegetarian; he often spoke of the need to limit personal requirements, to give to those in need the superfluous things with which we satisfy our whims. But his stormy, imperious nature would begin to murmur at this point, and his restless mind brought forth sharp objections.[43]

He even objected publicly to some of Tolstoy's ideas before the two of them formed their close relationship. He was annoyed by Tolstov's statements on women's education and nonresistance to evil, questions which, he said, "Tolstoy distorts like an idiot" (11.317). In an article of 1886 he cited the work of Russian nurses in the Crimean War as an example of what educated women could do in the way of "steadfast, firm, and persistent 'resistance' to evil" (11.323). Leskov was also scornful of many of Tolstoy's followers, seeing them as capable of little more than talk and drawing a parallel between them and the pseudo-nihilists of the sixties. He objected to Tolstoy's attacks on science, and to his denunciations of luxury. Fundamentally, the ascetic strain in Tolstoy's Christianity was quite alien to Leskov's epicurean love of life. As he once said to Gurevich: "He demands something which is beyond human nature, something impossible, impossible because such is our essence."[44] Leskov's attitude to Tolstoy thus reveals the dualism in his own personality: the intellectual demand to deny the passions and master the self which works against the emotional demand to satisfy the instinctive urgings of his own passionate nature.

VIII   *Leskov's Character and His Last Years*

A number of those who knew Leskov as an old man have left their impressions of him. What first struck visitors to the apartment where he spent his last years, 50 Furshtatskaya Street, was the writer's study, which so clearly reflected his own personality:

A visitor who entered the writer's study would usually find him reclining on a wide sofa or in a large armchair with his feet resting on another chair. The costume he wore at home — a sort of peculiar long woman's jacket or short dressinggown of bright striped fustian or some other material one would not expect to find used for this purpose — would momentarily con-strain him on the first acquaintance. He would excuse himself, although somehow rather hastily, and adjust his clothing, but immediately would forget about this and extend his hand to the visitor, scrutinizing him with eyes sparkling and full of curiosity. He truly loved to meet new people and grew animated on such occasions, becoming very talkative and quickly moving from topic to topic, touching on various major and minor events of the day, political or literary. He would speak out with passion, now angry, now sarcastic, now irritated, or, having hit upon an appropriate topic, he would provide a vivid story from his own life, full of the same odd and original words and phrases with which his works were filled but which in his vivacious speech burned with the dazzling splendor of jewels. He could talk on in this fashion for a whole evening. The numerous antique clocks which were arranged around the room and hung on its walls resounded every quarter-hour, now with the delicate tinkle of sleigh bells, now with a brief, ancient melody. Countless portraits, and paintings, both copies and originals, and an immense, long and narrow icon of the Virgin Mary hung on the middle of one wall with the icon-lamps swinging on chains before it — all this show of color from all sides before one's eyes aroused the imagination and disposed one to fantasy.[45]

Gurevich captures much of the personality of this difficult and contradictory man: his vivacity, curiosity, and interest in people; his love of words and the seemingly endless flow of anecdotes which made both his conversation and his writings fascinating; his love of rare objects of all sorts. But Leskov was more than a genial raconteur and connoisseur of rarities. His nervousness and impulsiveness, his irascibility, led him to hurt many people (although he often grew reconciled with them again) and gave him little peace of mind. Gurevich remarks that Leskov's blood must have contained a drop of the blood of Ivan the Terrible. "Not just a drop," adds Leskov's son, who had good reason to know, "but a sizable stream..."[46] Leskov found it difficult to adapt his prickly nature to the Christian teachings of charity and forgiveness which he espoused in his last years. "One must really treat me as a sick child," he wrote, "and allow me to damage and break those things which I myself love most of all. This is an indescribable condition, one which cannot be expressed in words; a fine mind, tormented by nerves. Heine called it 'toothache of the heart'. There is no cure; nothing on earth will work."[47] As he once confessed, "There is nowhere I can go because I must take myself with me everywhere, and for me that is the most disgusting burden."[48]

He spoke much of death in his final years, and apparently grew reconciled to it. "I believe in the immortality of the soul.... This world is a school which one must pass through and then be transferred to another class, perhaps a higher one, perhaps a lower one."[49] The angina with which he had suffered since 1889 tormented him, but its effects could be minimized if he avoided excitement. Given Leskov's inability to react dispassionately to much of anything, this was difficult. His son notes that a sudden knock at the door, a troublesome guest, or a newspaper article could irritate him sufficiently to cause an attack.

In February of 1895 he went to the Academy of Arts to view his portrait, painted by Valentin Serov the previous year. He was shocked when he saw the heavy dark frame around it, which appeared to him as the black border around an obituary. Several days later he contracted pneumonia after a drive through the Tauride Gardens. He died on February 21, 1895. Among the requests in his will were that his funeral be on the most modest scale possible, that his grave be marked only by a simple wooden cross, and that no eulogies be read at the graveside. "I know that I had very many bad qualities," he continued, "and that I deserve neither praise nor sympathy. He who wishes to censure me should realize that I first censured myself."[50]

CHAPTER 2

Early Stories and Drama

I *Early Peasant Stories*

LESKOV began his writing career as a journalist, treating popular topics in a deliberately fresh and controversial manner; his first efforts in fiction were also on a popular subject — the peasants — which he similarly approached from a consciously "different" point of view. Writers of the fifties and sixties had stressed the positive virtues of the peasant, attempting to evoke compassion for his hard lot and arouse indignation at the exploitation he endured from landowner and official. Although Leskov writes with obvious sympathy for the peasants, his image of their character is one of a core of violence covered in layers of ignorance. And he makes it clear that this view is based on his own intimate knowledge of his subject.

His first work of fiction, "Pogasshee delo" (A Cancelled Affair, 1862) leaves no doubt about the "darkness" of Russia's largest class. The peasants in the story are convinced that the ruinous drought in their village is somehow linked with the recent death of their sexton, and ask to have his body moved from the consecrated ground of the village cemetery. When the priest refuses, the peasants steal the body and, following the advice of a transient, burn a candle made of human fat as a means of ending the drought. The priest learns of the affair and manages to smooth it over while the peasants themselves remarkably keep silent about it for many years thereafter. The 1,000 villagers are portrayed as an unthinking, undifferentiated mass, easily led because they act only as a group and not as individuals. The story is significantly subtitled "From the Notes of my Grandfather," and appears to have had some factual basis (Leskov used a similar episode in another peasant story in 1892). Basing a work of fiction on an actual event, or at least making it appear as if based on fact, remained Leskov's most common manner of storytelling.

Two other peasant stories appear to have been intended as parts of a cycle involving a group of characters telling stories to each other while traveling to a fair, as in *The Canterbury Tales*, but dealing with peasant life in the manner of Turgenev's *Sportsman's Sketches*, a work which Leskov greatly admired. In the first, "Razboinik" (The Robber, 1862), Leskov describes all his characters in detail even though they do nothing but listen to the story. Thus it seems that he was preparing them to function in later stories. The peasant storyteller relates how once in the forest he encountered a ragged and starving runaway soldier who threatened him when he refused to give him bread. In panic the peasant struck the soldier, evidently killing him, and fled. This anecdote, however, takes up only about one-eighth of the volume of the story and is clearly not its center of interest. Leskov's approach is that of a journalist writing a sketch (*ocherk*) in which the "factual" element — character description, milieu, manners — outweighs the fictional. Leskov, like Turgenev, intends this "frame" to convey an overall atmosphere; unlike Turgenev, he fails to maintain one prevailing mood. Thus he goes to some lengths to create a sense of threatening disaster, although ultimately nothing very dreadful happens. This mood is disrupted toward the end when the narrator describes the snoring of his fellow travelers with truly Gogolian hyperbole, then further disrupted when the narrator relates his nightmare of the dying soldier in graphic detail. Such sudden shifts from humor to horror are typical of the early Leskov and indicative of his desire to achieve maximum impact with his material.

"V tarantase" (In the Tarantass, 1862) takes up the same journey on the following day, when the conversation of the travelers again turns to thievery and drunkenness. Two travelers each tell stories to explain the origins of these vices, and both express the belief that someday people will be able to live in unity and harmony. As in "The Robber," the frame takes up the greater part of the work. On the whole, this is a slight piece, although it does show Leskov's concern with religion as a means of combating evil.

Leskov's insights into the peasant mentality are amusingly expressed in "Iazvitel'nyi" (The Stinger, 1863). The narrator, a civil servant, is assigned to investigate peasants' complaints against a new English overseer, Deane. Neighboring landowners testify that

Deane is an excellent manager who never flogs the peasants and who does not demand much work from them. Yet they burn down his house, beat him, and drive him away. Eventually the narrator learns that their grievance arises from the humane form of punishment devised by the enlightened overseer. Exasperated by the drunkenness and unreliability of one peasant and unwilling to resort to corporal punishment, Deane ties a thread to him "like a sparrow" and forces him to sit on a chair where the others can see him. The peasants absolutely refuse to have any further dealings with Deane because "he's a stinger." They accept trial, flogging, and exile rather than suffer further humiliation. Here Leskov first touches a theme which runs throughout his work — the idealist who comes to grief when he encounters the elemental nature of the Russian peasant and the hard facts of Russian life.

Such a figure appears in "Ovtsebyk" (The Musk-ox, 1862), the most ambitious of Leskov's earliest stories. Vasily Petrovich, the first of Leskov's eccentrics, is nicknamed "musk-ox" because of his unmannerly gruffness and because of the shaggy locks of hair which hang down over each ear. Yet beneath this gruff exterior hides an almost saintly creature who lives with truly "evangelical lack of concern for himself" (1. 32) and a willingness to sacrifice himself for a worthy ideal. Deeply moved by the injustices he sees around him, Vasily Petrovich rejects the priesthood for which he has studied and becomes an agitator, moving about the country vainly trying to stir up revolutionary sentiments among the sectarians and peasants. For a time he works for an ex-peasant entrepreneur named Sviridov and tries to rouse Sviridov's peasants, but they are only amused by his harangues. Vasily Petrovich, in despair that he cannot put his ideals into practice, eventually hangs himself.

Vasily Petrovich is a characteristic Leskovian figure, totally at odds with the standards and values of his day. His opposition to the existing order which leads him to revolutionary agitation comes not from the theories circulating in the early 1860s (he despises these) but from the only works he reads — the Gospels and classical literature, particularly Plato. He is an idealist whose ideals are shattered when they collide with real life.

The story scarcely endeared Leskov to the literary radicals of his day since it went against the grain of many of their most cherished beliefs. The Old Believers with whom Vasily Petrovich lives for a time appear as ultraconservative obscurantists who only want to live by the letter of their beliefs, not as a potential force of opposition to the regime. The peasants likewise are unreceptive and even hostile to Vasily Petrovich's ideas. The one figure who does express positive ideas and manages to put them into practice is Sviridov, the self-made capitalist. Sviridov plays a minor role in the story, but it is clear that he is intended as a foil to Vasily Petrovich. While Vasily Petrovich comes to the conclusion that for him there is "nowhere to go" (*nekuda idti*), Sviridov's individual initiative and enterprise provide a more general solution. Leskov certainly does not condemn his musk-ox — indeed, he admires him — but simply shows that his idealism is out of touch with reality.

"Zhitie odnoi baby" (The Life of a Peasant Woman, 1863) combines the *ocherk* form and its detailed descriptions of peasant life with an account of the tragic love of its heroine, Nastya. She is a beautiful girl whose enterprising but totally unscrupulous brother forces her to marry the weak-minded son of his business partner. Nastya appears to be meek and has something of an artistic nature, but she is also an uncompromising idealist. She is horrified by the idea of marriage to her repulsive suitor but can do nothing to prevent it. Her married life eventually drives her to hysteria and epileptic seizures. A kindly old healer, Krylushkin, undertakes to treat her. After her recovery she begins a love affair with Stepan, a married peasant. When she discovers that she is pregnant, she flees with her lover, but without passports the two are soon captured. Stepan's child is born prematurely in prison and dies, as does Stepan himself. Nastya is again driven to the verge of insanity by this accumulation of disasters and returns to Krylushkin. But the local authorities decide that Krylushkin's methods of treatment, although successful, must be stopped because they have not been officially sanctioned. Their harsh treatment of Nastya during a search of Krylushkin's house again drives her to a frenzy. She is taken to an asylum, escapes, and freezes to death in the forest.

Leskov tells the story in memoir form (it is subtitled "From my Gostomlya Recollections") and treats peasant life and lore in detail, describing peasant houses, wedding customs, work habits, and including a whole series of folk songs (both Nastya and Stepan are talented singers). The songs are nicely integrated into the story and almost summarize its plot. They also reveal Nastya's and Stepan's talent and capacity for deep feeling which sets them apart from the rest of the villagers. But the story is marred by its uneven tone and structure. Some passages — the joyless wedding cere-

mony, for example — are almost tragic; others, such as the description of the death of Nastya's child, are sentimentalized and pathetic. The plot begins to unfold in a leisurely fashion until the sudden
rush of incidents toward the end: the flight of the two lovers, their
arrest, the birth and death of Nastya's child, Stepan's death, and
Nastya's insanity, recovery, and renewed insanity all occur within
the last three chapters. The narrator's language also undergoes a
change: he begins in the folksy style of a small Gostomlya landowner but drops this mask in the latter part of the work to narrate
in a more neutral style.[1]

Leskov again stresses the darker side of the peasant character,
portraying many scenes of physical violence and sexual passion.
Kostik, Nastya's brother, is obsessed with money and is a drunkard
and profligate. The villagers as a whole are readily prone to violence, lust, and drunkenness. Even the story's one saintly figure,
Krylushkin, is rumored to have driven his wife to an early grave
before a religious conversion led him to become a healer. The epilogue wherein the narrator returns to Gostomlya five years later
(and after the Emancipation) makes an important point about this:
freeing the peasants from the power of the landowners has done
nothing to enlighten them, for the strong still tyrannize over the
weak. The few glimmers of enlightenment that are visible seem all
but lost in the overpowering darkness of village life. Children are
learning to read, for example, but when the narrator gives a book
to one particularly bright boy, the boy soon returns it since the
other children have beaten him in envy. The practice of *snok-
hachestvo* — the cohabitation of father-in-law and daughter-in-law
— continues, as do bribery and oppression, not of peasants by
landowners but of peasants by peasants. The reform of an evil institution had not eliminated the real evil, which lies deeper within
human nature. Leskov is clearly taking issue with the radicals and
liberals who, without sufficient knowledge of the peasants, assumed that all of the evils of village life were due to serfdom. (His
narrator pointedly remarks that he returned to Gostomlya to reexamine peasant life for himself since he did not recognize it as it
was portrayed in literature.) He ends the story, however, with a
conversation with a landowner's young son who is full of enthusi-
asm for teaching peasant children and who quotes a verse from
Apollon Maykov pleading for spiritual nourishment for Russia.

Leskov's first efforts in fiction were marked by the same spirit of
polemic and iconoclasm as had been his early journalism. He

scornfully dismissed previous treatments of the peasant in literature, exempting only Turgenev's and Ostrovsky's works from what
he saw as "artificial and improbable" stories about "paysans" (11.
12). Thus he creates a narrator with an intimate knowledge of
village life who neither patronizes nor idealizes the peasants. His
view of the peasantry as lost in ignorance and totally uncompre-
hending of those who seek to reform them or rouse them to action
clashed sharply with the views of the radical intellectuals, who were
already beginning to create their cult of the people. Leskov's peasants are primitives; they react physically, often violently, and not
as individuals but as a group. Those high-minded characters such
as the "musk-ox" and Deane, the English overseer, who, blinded
by preconceived notions, fail to take the real character of the
peasants into account, meet disaster. In spite of some obvious influences (Gogol and Turgenev in particular), Leskov's stories already
achieve a distinctive form. They do not readily fit into the more
common genres of short story or tale: they blend fiction with personal reminiscence or other factual elements; they rely heavily on
an individualized narrator telling his story in a distinctive language;
their plots are often subordinated to peripheral incident or description of milieu.

II   *Three Tales*

In Leskov's novel *No Way Out* a group of characters discuss
peasant life and its portrayal in literature. Rozanov, a doctor with a
broad knowledge of Russian life, tells of a young peasant woman
who calmly and without reflection murdered her unfaithful husband. "But this isn't drama," counters Zarnitsyn, a teacher. "How
could you portray that on the stage? You can't present any moral
conflict here because it is all coarse and happens so abruptly. There
is no struggle at all; the matter is simply decided. When the life of
the people is like that there isn't any drama, nor can there be; there
are criminal cases but certainly no drama" (2. 180). Zarnitsyn
argues that art has its own particular rules which would exclude the
kind of events mentioned by Rozanov. "What do they care for
your art and its rules," objects Rozanov. Peasant life has conflict
enough, "But we don't know how to talk about that conflict" (2.
180). He tells several more stories to support his argument, all
stressing the direct and uncompromising nature of the Russians
which would give their drama a unique flavor.

"Ledi Makbet mtsenskogo uezda" (Lady Macbeth of Mtsensk, 1865) is a concrete example supporting Rozanov's views. Leskov's title not only underlines the strong will of his title figure, it also elevates her to the status of a tragic heroine. Rozanov's scorn for the accepted rules of art reflects Leskov's desire to introduce new themes and techniques into literature, to find a suitable approach to the drama of Russian life.

The story is among Leskov's most memorable ones. The drama of the young peasant girl Katerina Izmaylova, trapped in a sterile marriage to an aging merchant, moves with a genuinely tragic sense of inevitability as she takes a lover, Sergey, and commits a series of murders in order to keep him. The most chilling aspect of the story is not the graphic accounts of four murders but the fact that Katerina, portrayed as a beautiful but otherwise unexceptional girl, is able to commit her acts so calmly, with little apparent remorse. There seems indeed to be no moral struggle.

Leskov's epigraph, "The first song is sung with a blush," gives a clue to her behavior. The first murder happens almost logically: her father-in-law has discovered her liaison with Sergey and threatens to expose her and have her lover arrested. But her passion for Sergey after five years of loveless marriage is so strong that she loses sight of all else. The second murder occurs simply because she must dispose of her husband, who has also discovered her affair. Her third crime is less spontaneous but still motivated by her passion for Sergey. A distant relative, a boy, turns up to claim part of her late husband's estate. Sergey grumbles that their future is no longer secure because of this new claimant, and she obliges by murdering the boy as well. One can perhaps argue that her husband and father-in-law have only received their just desserts, but the boy is innocent of any ill will toward Katerina. Leskov heightens the emotional impact of this third murder by describing it in considerably more detail than the others.

Had the story ended here, with the discovery of the murders and the arrest of Katerina and Sergey, it would have proven Zarnitsyn's point that there may be criminal cases but little drama in Russian life. But Leskov continues with the convicts' journey to Siberia. It is here that Katerina becomes not just a murderess, but a tragic heroine. Sergey, for whose sake she has committed three murders, now loses interest in her once his chance to enrich himself has passed, and openly carries on with another female prisoner, Sonetka. Katerina responds in her usual uncompromising way by

murdering her rival and killing herself. It is only in this latter part
of the story that we see Katerina suffer, though not from remorse,
but simply from pain at the loss of her lover.

Much of the peculiar effect of the story arises from the absence
of any direct inner views of Katerina. A tense and powerful drama
such as this usually brings with it some analysis of the character's
psyche to help explain her motivations. Leskov, however, suggests
that Katerina is too uncomplicated an individual to allow for much
fine psychological analysis. Instead he most vividly conveys her
physical presence, and only indirectly, through a number of telling
details, suggests something of her inner life as well. The stifling atmosphere of her husband's household ("that Russian boredom, the
boredom of a merchant's house, enough, as they say, to make even
hanging oneself a pleasure," [1. 98]) is evoked by recurring images
of windows and doors alternately confining her and giving release.
(A crowd peering through the closed shutters of the house discovers
her in the act of her third murder.) The bursting of the mill dam
which motivates her husband's absence is also an expressive meta-
phor for the accumulation and release of her passion. Leskov uses
her first encounter with Sergey to suggest her amazing inner
strength of character which so contrasts with her outward frailty.
Sergey is surprised at how little she weighs, but an old peasant remarks: "Your body, young man, is nothing on the scale: it is your
strength that counts and not the body!" (1. 99). The fat, fluffy cat
appearing in her dreams symbolizes the awakened sensuality which
now drives her; the cat's second appearance, now with the head of
her murdered father-in-law, suggests her guilty conscience. These
and other details add a psychological dimension which might not be
immediately apparent in the story. Leskov's deliberate use of this
rather primitive means of conveying psychology is in keeping with
his subject's primitive nature and is, as Doctor Rozanov noted, an
appropriate language for describing such a moral conflict. The
blend of fine lyricism with coarse detail in the passage of the close
of chapter 6 (Katerina and Sergey are making love under an apple
tree) captures the ambiguous nature of the heroine, herself compounded of delicacy and animal passion:

Katerina Lvovna, bathed in moonlight and rolling on the soft carpet,
frisked and played with her husband's young clerk. And the new white
blossoms from the bushy apple tree kept falling and falling on them until
at last they ceased to fall. Meanwhile the short summer night had passed,

the moon hid herself behind the steep, high roofs of the warehouses and looked at the earth ever more wanly; a piercing feline duet came from the kitchen roof; then someone spat and snorted angrily after which two or three tomcats crashed noisily from the roof onto a pile of boards nearby. (1. 112)

"Lady Macbeth" was planned as the first in a cycle of twelve sketches about women from various social levels (10. 253). The cycle never materialized, but "Voitel'nitsa" (The Amazon, 1866) was likely conceived as another of its members. It too is subtitled a "sketch," and centers on the unhappy love affair of a woman of strong character. Although it has other similarities to "Lady Macbeth," "The Amazon" represents a new departure toward what was to become one of Leskov's major concerns. This is the first of a number of "St. Petersburg" stories, almost all of which are strongly satirical. The setting here is even more important than the Gostomlya of the earlier stories; indeed it is central to the meaning of the work. Here too, for the first time, Leskov achieves a genuine linguistic *tour de force*.

The story's structure seems rather odd at first: almost all of the plot is related in one lengthy chapter; another chapter chronicles a series of incidents in the life of the heroine; and five short chapters serve as introduction, transition, and epilogue. But this seemingly awkward structure has its own logic which eventually becomes clear. The first two chapters sketch the character of the heroine, Domna Platonovna, who has been transplanted from a merchant family of Mtsensk to the capital where — nominally at least — she is a seller of lace. But this only provides a pretext for admission into St. Petersburg families so that she may carry out all sorts of tasks which the respectable bourgeois are unwilling to do for themselves. She buys and sells old furniture and clothes, but most of her business concerns matters of the heart. Thus she arranges marriages, finds suitable mistresses for elderly gentlemen, and effectively sells impoverished young provincial ladies into prostitution. She is a professional busybody whose contacts with all levels of St. Petersburg society have opened her eyes and given her, in her own words, a complete understanding of "Petersburg circumstances." Although she considers everyone she meets to be a scoundrel, she makes an exception for people from Orel province, and thus confides in the narrator. She relates to him the principal plot line of the story, the history of her dealings with Lekanida, a young woman of

Polish descent who has been reduced to destitution after leaving her husband. Domna Platonovna takes pity on Lekanida and goes to great pains to "put her on the right path" by finding a willing buyer for her favors. She is baffled by Lekanida's reluctance to be "reformed," but when Lekanida in desperation finally succumbs and becomes the mistress of a general, Domna Platonovna is deeply hurt by her protégée's ingratitude.

Domna Platonovna then proceeds to pour out a seemingly endless flow of anecdotes illustrating the rascally nature of the people of St. Petersburg. Her case is a good one: she tells in her own vivid fashion of the deceit of cabdrivers and generals' wives. All this was in the past, however; now she understands "Petersburg circumstances" and is no longer taken in. This, indeed, is the main point of the story and gives it its satirical bite: Domna Platonovna is, in her way, simple and forthright in that she sees what really motivates the behavior of Petersburgers — selfishness, lust, and greed. She accepts this and acts on the basis of the real, rather than the professed, values of her society. Thus she really does feel pity for Lekanida and sincerely believes that she is saving her by selling her into prostitution. Lekanida, struggling to resist, cries out in despair: "Where are the compassionate, good Christians? Where are they? Where?" "Why here," Domna replies. "Where?" "What do you mean, *where*? The whole of Russia is Christian, and you and I are Christians" (1. 180).

The city itself appears almost alive, nourishing an active malevolence toward its inhabitants. The narrator describes his unwilling return to the capital after a five-year absence, when he must again "listen to its incessant din, regard its pale, worried and spent faces, breathe the stench of its fumes, and brood under the dispiriting impression of its tubercular white nights"[2] (1. 190). And Leskov makes it plain that the city has worked its way on Domna Platonovna: "At first she humbly trudged about with her lace and thought not at all of combining this trade with any other activities. But the Enchantress Capital transformed this absurd, simple woman of Mtsensk into the subtle factotum I came to know in our precious Domna Platonovna" (1. 151). The city has indeed created her as a necessary agent to carry out the dirty work of a corrupt society. And Domna Platonovna never lacks work.

The narrator's attitude toward Domna Platonovna is less unequivocal than is his view of the city. Her own account of her career appears to condemn her as one both totally corrupted and busily corrupting all within her reach. Significantly, the narrator first meets her as he hears his landlady recite a verse by the Polish poet Antoni Malczewski: "Because death destroys all on this earth. And even in the magnificent rose nests the worm." And Domna Platonovna enters. But the layer of cynicism which has enabled Domna Platonovna to cope with Petersburg circumstances does not run very deep; at heart she is still a good woman with a genuine concern for people. She suffers as much from circumstances as do Leskov's earlier heroines. Certainly the ending of the story shows her more as a victim than a villain. The narrator finds her several years after their first meeting working as an attendant at a charity hospital. She has now lost her former verve and vitality and is a broken woman at forty-seven. After having arranged so many "marriages" with such apparent cynicism, she had herself fallen hopelessly in love with a thorough scoundrel more than twenty years her junior. When her lover is arrested for theft, she wastes away and dies.

Apart from its nice irony, the ending may seem abrupt and yet it is hardly surprising that she who has denied passion should fall its victim. Most of her adventures have some erotic shading. Once she sleeps with the father of her godchild (*kum*), thinking he is her husband. On another occasion, having imbibed too much at a lady friend's, she spends the night in her friend's bed, after which she takes to sewing herself into her bedclothes when sleeping away from home (she is an exceptionally sound sleeper). One of her dreams is particularly interesting: she is approached by a tiny man, "not much bigger than a rooster; a teeny-tiny face, in a little blue caftan, and he's holding a little green peaked cap on his head. 'Come on, Domochka,' he says, 'Let's you and I make love'" (1. 210–11). She rejects him as too small but the whole night she is besieged by tiny devils who beat upon her stomach like a drum — "bum — burum — bum." These episodes from her "discontinuous life" are the farcical counterpart to Katerina Izmaylova's unacknowledged sensuality; the release of this passion leads to Domna's ruin as well.

The story is Leskov's first extended *skaz*,[3] and he excels himself in its language. Domna Platonovna narrates the bulk of it in her unique blend of Mtsensk merchant speech with highfalutin St. Petersburg vocabulary. Coarse invective alternates with affectionate diminutives, elevated archaisms with earthy popular expressions. Her language truly makes her come alive; its irrepressible

flow conveys her vitality and her inherently "busy" nature. The
narrative technique used here — the garrulous, "unaware" storyteller whose candid affirmation of twisted values exposes what her
society lives by but never acknowledges — foreshadows that of
Leskov's trenchant satires of the 1890s.

The third story of this period, "Kotin doilets i Platonida" (Kotin
the Provider[4] and Platonida) is weaker than the two earlier ones because it lacks their unified effect. Leskov originally wrote it as an
episode in his unfinished novel, *Chaiushchie dvizheniia vody*
(Waiting for the Moving of the Water, the future *Cathedral Folk*),
then published it independently in a collection of stories in 1867
and finally added an ending (chapter 6) for his *Collected Works* in
1890. Although it never manages to conceal its patchwork quality,
it is noteworthy because it contains Leskov's first truly positive
hero.

The hero, Konstantin Pizonsky, was raised in a nunnery as a girl
until the age of twelve, and never manages to overcome his uncer-
tainty about his real sex, often referring to himself using the feminine forms. His absurd appearance and peculiar manners make him
the butt of the ridicule of his schoolmasters, and he is soon expelled
as a hopeless case. (The name Kotin arose when, in panic at a teacher's request that he write his name, he wrote "Konstantintintintin-
tin," and when asked to correct this, curbed his graphomania by
writing only "Kotin.") Kotin eventually adopts two orphaned
nieces to save them from a life as beggars and, although he himself
does not have a roof over his head, devotes himself to their upbringing. He is ingenious and industrious, and soon becomes indis-
pensable as the town's jack-of-all-trades. In time he is allowed to
live on a deserted island in the river which he transforms into a
flourishing garden. Kotin has been assisted in his child-rearing by
Platonida, a young woman unhappily married to the eldest son of
Kotin's uncle, an Old Believer merchant. Platonida is attracted to
Avenir, her brother-in-law, but resists Avenir's advances. She is relieved when her husband dies unexpectedly and rejoices briefly in her
new freedom. But the night of the funeral her father-in-law forces
his way into her room and attempts to rape her. She strikes him
with an ax and flees, believing she has killed him. He is only slightly
hurt, however, and explains her absence by charging her and Avenir
with attempting to rob and murder him. Pizonsky is imprisoned
for a time on suspicion of harboring her but is soon released. Platonida retreats to a nunnery and lives out her days in blindness.

Pizonsky is the first of Leskov's self-sacrificing, absurd heroes who, unlike his "Musk-ox," manages to achieve something positive. By creating a figure of ridiculous appearance and ambiguous sex, Leskov manages to avoid sentimentalizing him, a pitfall he did not always escape in other works. Pizonsky's ambiguous sexuality is a frequent trait of Leskov's positive heroes: they are often sexless beings, untroubled by passion and capable of maternal warmth and love. The absurdity of Pizonsky's behavior is one of his positive virtues: when Pizonsky takes on the task of raising his nieces, Leskov stresses that he acts directly on the basis of his feelings. Common sense would tell him that he has every reason not to concern himself with the fate of the girls, but since he is a fool who cannot even write his own name, he is not troubled by common sense. Pizonsky is also enterprising and applies his talents so well that he is soon able to live independently. Leskov calls him a Robinson Crusoe, not only because he lives on an island, but also because he is able to create a comfortable life for himself using his own ingenuity and the materials at hand. He is, after all, a man of talent (Leskov calls him an artist), another trait of Leskov's positive heroes.

Platonida's story only briefly touches Pizonsky's, and its point is apparently in the contrast it provides with it. Pizonsky has two children and a happy family life with them; Platonida is childless and trapped in a loveless marriage. Pizonsky is passionless, channeling all his love toward his children; she has no outlet for the passion which she herself only begins to acknowledge. In some of the best pages of Platonida's story — the scene of his heroine in her bedroom after her husband's funeral — Leskov succeeds wonderfully in conveying her inner drama with little psychological analysis simply by fitting together a series of suggestive images, as he did in "Lady Macbeth." Platonida suddenly becomes aware of her new freedom and of both the force and consequences of the bottled-up passion within her. She devours a bunch of grapes offered to her by Avenir, gazes with fascination at the doves kissing on the rooftops outside her window, then notices: "In the very middle of the dead Marko's pillow, which his mischievous widow had thrown on the floor, was a small depression as if someone invisible had laid his head there. At the top of this hollow, in the place where the portrait of the Savior would be on the crown worn by the deceased, sat a gray moth. It sat, raised up on its thin legs, slowly opening and closing its wings, just as if it were an ascetic monk raising his robe to make the sign of the cross over the open grave. Platonida shuddered'' (1. 255).

Despite a few effective scenes such as this (Leskov's portrayal of the senile lust of Platonida's father-in-law is also impressive), the two separate stories are not linked tightly enough to give the tale full impact.

These three stories, then, not only mark the maturation of Leskov's talent, but also point out the three main lines along which he continued to work: the tale of strong passions and absorbing incident, such as ''Lady Macbeth''; the slyly satirical tale, often accompanied by verbal virtuosity presenting, as it were, the negative aspects of Leskov's fictional world; and the positive values exemplified by his first ''righteous man,'' Pizonsky.

III   *Leskov and the Drama*

In the late 1860s Leskov devoted himself to another very topical question, the state of the theater in St. Petersburg. In a series of newspaper and journal articles he commented on the poverty of the theatrical repertoire and the lamentable state of the acting profession, and called for fresh talents to revive the theater. His theatrical reviews are not especially penetrating, his chief complaint being that current plays were boring, but the works he reviewed were hardly distinguished either. Through his own melodrama, *Rastochitel'* (The Wastrel), which premiered on November 1, 1867, he attempted to inject fresh life into the theater.

The Wastrel centers on the schemes of an archvillain, Knyazev, a merchant and the most powerful man in a provincial town. Knyazev has managed the affairs of another young merchant, Molchanov. Eventually we learn that Knyazev had murdered Molchanov's father years earlier after arranging a will giving him trusteeship over young Molchanov's affairs. Knyazev has squandered 200,000 rubles of the entrusted money and is about to be called to account by the newly reformed lawcourts. Knyazev is a master of intrigue, however, and manages to rally the town's leading citizens against Molchanov. They have Molchanov declared an irresponsible wastrel, allowing Knyazev to continue his trusteeship and hide his crimes. When Molchanov attempts to go to St. Petersburg to fight his case, Knyazev has him committed to an asylum as a madman. Here Molchanov does in fact go insane but manages to escape and, in a frenzy, sets fire to the town and dies of burns. The play also has a romantic interest. Knyazev has arranged to marry Molchanov to a woman he despises and who takes sides against him. Marina, Molchanov's childhood sweetheart (for whom Knyazev has also arranged an unhappy marriage) becomes the object of rivalry between Molchanov and Knyazev. In the true style of a stage heroine, she resists Knyazev's advances and ultimately poisons herself rather than submit to him.

Molchanov, a man who wishes only to do good but who is set upon by villains, is the play's hero, and his dilemma should arouse the sympathy and righteous indignation of the audience. Leskov intends him to be a complex character, a good man who falls prey to his strong passions. As he admits, "I do not fear my enemies, I fear only myself" (1. 410). And Leskov does show that Molchanov's downfall is due as much to his own flaws as to Knyazev's machinations. His furious outburst when Knyazev proposes to reinstate trusteeship helps convince the townspeople that he is indeed irresponsible. Molchanov also wishes to improve conditions for his workers and decides to raise their pay. But this causes an uproar among the other merchants of the town, who claim they will be driven to bankruptcy in trying to match Molchanov's wage level. Thus the merchants are only too willing to be led by Knyazev into declaring Molchanov incompetent. But Molchanov is never on stage long enough to allow the audience to understand his motivations and to establish himself as a convincing character. The action is totally dominated by Knyazev, who manipulates Molchanov so readily that the latter emerges as a naive and helpless figure. Knyazev himself is an interesting character, but his villany is so extreme and tinged with sadism that it is difficult to believe in him. "I do sometimes love to see women weeping," he says, "when they weep their lips are so . . . hot, and they're aquiver like a butterfly on a pin. How long it's been since I kissed a woman like that!" (1. 392).

The play's framework — from the opening disclosure that Knyazev is to be called to account for his misdeeds, to the closing when, at his moment of triumph, he learns that the courts have again taken up his case — owes much to Gogol's *Inspector-General*. But Leskov makes it plain that Knyazev will circumvent justice in the end. Leskov's portrayal of evil in provincial Russia lacks, of course, the grotesque humor of a Gogol. Leskov deals with the surface appearance of evil without Gogol's metaphysical dimension. As in his previous prose writings, Leskov relies here on a number of calculated effects designed to sustain interest. Among the characters

is a "holy fool," Alyosha, a former merchant who witnessed Knyazev's murder of Molchanov's father and who has gone mad.
Alyosha appears at several appropriate times and causes the usually
cool Knyazev to lose his equilibrium momentarily, but he has
almost no other function in the play. Act 4, the slowest, contains
several long monologues whose purpose is simply to delay Molchanov's departure for St. Petersburg so that Knyazev can seize
him. Leskov enlivens this act with songs, dancing, and comic dialogue with extensive wordplay. The melodrama climaxes in the last
act as we witness simultaneously Marina's death throes, Molchanov's body being dragged on the stage, and the town in flames in the
background.

The absorbing plot, striking effects, and larger-than-life characters gave the play a measure of success in provincial theaters. Reviewers in the capital were almost uniformly hostile, however,
though their indignation was directed more at Leskov's supposed
attitudes toward the current judicial reforms than at any flaws in
the play. The reforms were warmly welcomed by liberal opinion
and Leskov himself approved of the new courts. His point in the
play, however, is that the evil in individuals runs far too deep to be
corrected only through legislation. Knyazev in fact uses the new
laws to maintain his power over Molchanov. He dismisses the
power of the new courts by saying, "I cannot believe that a man of
wit should not do as he pleases in Russia" (1. 388). Reviewers saw
in Knyazev's easy manipulation of the townspeople an expression
of Leskov's hostility to the judicial reforms and toward the very
idea of local self-government. And in fact there is a strong element
of scorn for the mob which so readily gives its assent to Knyazev's
proposals. It was an unflattering view of society, but one which
perhaps was closer to the truth than Leskov's critics cared to admit.
The positive message that emerges from the play is that the individual's duty is to resist evil by standing up for his rights and asserting
his independence. As one of the characters in the play remarks,
"An honest man in Russia is an expert at keeping his mouth shut
just when he ought not to keep his mouth shut" (1. 412).

Leskov completed no more plays, although his archives contains
some notes for a projected drama.[5] He continued to write drama
reviews until 1871, however, and never lost interest in the theater.

CHAPTER 3

Novels and Chronicles

I Early Novels

RUSSIAN writers at mid-century were largely judged by their talent as novelists, so it was to be expected that the ambitious and energetic Leskov should turn to larger genres once he had made his mark in short fiction. The novel in Russia had, by the mid-1860s, become a powerful vehicle for social comment, and Leskov had a number of comments to make about his society. Thus he conceived his first novel, *No Way Out*, as a summing up of the whole stormy era of the 1860s and it created a sizable storm of its own.

It is an ambitious work: its three books — "In the Provinces," "In Moscow," and "On the Banks of the Neva" — respectively deal with life in Russia's three principal "settings" and touch upon the major issues of the era. It also has three plot lines which begin together but soon diverge, touching only occasionally thereafter. Leskov's main heroine, Liza Bakhareva, returns to her provincial home after completing her studies and immediately rebels against her family's tedious and confining way of life. Liza is proud, idealistic, and intelligent, but has no patience with the idle and superficial people around her. She seeks escape in voracious reading and withdraws into herself. When her family moves to Moscow she finds some solace in an "advanced" liberal circle led by a flighty Marquise, but is quickly disillusioned and joins the nihilist movement in St. Petersburg. Eventually she settles in a newly established commune (modeled on the pattern set out in *What is to be Done?*) only to discover that its members are as superficial and petty as the people from whom she has fled.[1] Totally disillusioned and convinced that there is no way out of her dilemma, she dies of pneumonia.

The second heroine, Jenny Glovatskaya, plays a much smaller role in the novel. She studied with Liza and returns to the provinces where, like her classmate, she is dismayed by the stifling atmosphere in which she must live. But Jenny's character is much milder than Liza's, and she accepts people and circumstances as she finds them. She marries an ambitious provincial schoolteacher, and in St. Petersburg at the novel's end uneasily watches her husband's idealism wither as his career flourishes. Doctor Rozanov, the third hero, often acts as Leskov's mouthpiece. He is a skeptic and an independent thinker with a large measure of common sense and broad practical experience. Rozanov also flees from provincial life and from an unhappy marriage. His interest in a group of Moscow revolutionaries quickly fades when he realizes that they are either fools or scoundrels. Later, in St. Petersburg, he can only look on helplessly as Liza is drawn further into the nihilist movement.

Leskov not only caricatures the radicals as individuals but also, through Rozanov, challenges their ideas and derides their reliance on dogma as a guide to cures for Russia's ills. Theories, Rozanov argues, are a Procrustean bed to which circumstances are adapted; they are restrictive and do not allow for the freedom and independence of the individual. "My theory," he says, "is to live independently from theories and not step on anyone's toes" (2.185). This anti-ideological, anti-dogmatic stance is reflected in the plot of the novel as well. As Liza seeks some meaning for her life by relying solely on abstractions, she loses a measure of her humanity, grows totally self-centered, and spurns those who are devoted to her. She lives only for the future, for the day when, according to theory, the revolution will reorganize society and allow her to be free and happy. But when it becomes clear to her that she will not see this day, her life loses its meaning. The other nihilists — whom Leskov portrays as being totally out of touch with Russian life — have also based their hopes on Russia's potential for revolution and undergo a similar process of disillusionment. Rozanov's skepticism about the possibility of revolution arises not from theory but from his knowledge of conditions in the countryside and the mentality of the peasant.

No Way Out thus fits into the tradition of anti-nihilist novels of the sixties.[2] But the novel is by no means a wholesale denunciation of all those who seek social change. To be sure, Leskov gleefully heaps abuse on the superficial pseudo-nihilists with their uncritical acceptance of current radical clichés and on the cynical hangers-on who use the movement to further their own selfish ends. But he does make an earnest attempt to show why intelligent and talented young people such as Liza Bakhareva are attracted to the movement and does portray them with some sympathy. It is clear that Leskov intends his readers to respect her history as an honest quest for truth by an uncompromising, if overly idealistic, young woman. Indeed, Rozanov himself could be called a nihilist insofar as he regards so-called "truths" with a healthy skepticism based on personal experience and is a firm believer in practical work as a solution to Russia's ills. Another respectable revolutionary is Rayner, whom Leskov modeled on his friend Artur Benni.[3] Rayner is of Swiss and Russian parentage, and his father's family had a tradition of revolutionary and socialist activities. Raised abroad, he grows disenchanted with European civilization and travels to Russia, expecting to find, as Russian emigrés have insisted, that Russian peasants are by nature inclined to socialism and ripe for revolution. The vast network of dedicated revolutionaries he expected would lead an uprising turns out to be a small band of squabbling and hopelessly disorganized phrasemongers. Like Liza, Rayner is a highminded idealist, but so naive that he allows himself to be shamelessly exploited by the nihilists. He, too, is disillusioned and joins the Polish uprising until he is captured by the Russians and executed. Rayner is clearly intended as a symbolic figure. Leskov goes to some length to describe his roots in the European socialist and revolutionary tradition and makes his point when Rayner's attempt to transplant this alien tradition in Russian soil fails miserably.

Leskov provides very little in the way of a positive program. His three main characters have each reached a dead end at the conclusion of the novel. One of the final scenes is a gathering at Jenny Glovatskaya's which makes it clear that society is still preoccupied with the same frivolities which caused Liza to try to change it. The last pages, which have the air of being hurriedly tacked on, return the setting to the provinces and introduce a new character, Luka Maslyannikov. He is a merchant's son who deliberately turns his back on the intellectual life of the cities and quietly practices efficient, large-scale agriculture. Leskov thus takes one parting shot at the radicals, who are wasting their energies in futile debate while a new generation of entrepreneurs is making real progress. He is also attempting to complete the geographical movement of the novel by returning it firmly to the soil of the provinces after the airy heights of Moscow and St. Petersburg.

The flaws in the novel are many. Leskov clearly uses it to settle personal scores and so creates a host of caricatures: unconvincing, one-dimensional characters who often have scant relation to the plot. In his efforts to intrigue his readers he resorts to much needless mystification (his fascination for describing old, mysterious houses no doubt derives from the Gothic novel). The work's construction is generally untidy: Jenny, a major figure in book 1, is ignored until the novel's end; a tangle of peripheral incidents and characters often obscures the plot in books 2 and 3. Leskov was trying to paint a detailed portrait of his age and thus was anxious not to omit anything, but such shaky construction is typical of his novels.

Contemporary critics were so incensed by Leskov's attacks on living people that they ignored what artistic merit the work does have. In spite of its tendentiousness, it does examine the major issues of the 1860s. If at times it strains one's credulity, it does have many absorbing and dramatic scenes and much keen, often vicious, humor. If many characters are overdrawn, at least Liza and Rozanov are portrayed with care and insight. In later years Leskov took pride in his novel and considered it the work which depicted the 1860s most faithfully.[4] And certainly it conveys the flavor of the era in its survey of topical issues: women's emancipation; marriage and the family; communal life; the establishment of the first revolutionary organizations; the liberal's flirtation with revolution; the intrigues of Polish nationalists in Russia; the attitude of the emigrés toward the situation in Russia; the dilemma of many young idealists who found that their society indeed left them with no channels for their strivings.

After the furor around *No Way Out* is not surprising that Leskov should devote himself to a novel which, he was careful to assure a prospective editor, was "not at all tendentious" (10.256). In *Oboidennye* (The By-Passed, 1865) Leskov writes about private rather than public matters; he portrays "little people," those bypassed by the major novelists of the day. As he remarks:

The reader need not expect to encounter here either the heroes of Russian progress nor savage reactionaries. In this novel there will be neither country schoolteachers who open inexpensive libraries for illiterate peasants, nor husbands who subsidize the lovers of their wives who have run off, nor beds of nails on which exemplary people somehow are able to sleep, nor tyrannical fathers who specially concern themselves with oppressing their brilliant children. . . . In short, there will not be a single civic hero here; but there will be people with weaknesses, people who have been badly brought up.[5]

Leskov stresses his detachment from the concerns of the day by setting much of his novel outside Russia and by creating a hero who is very definitely not part of the mainstream of life in the 1860s. In deliberate contrast to the heroes of the "progressive" novels which Leskov sarcastically dismisses above, his hero — Nestor Dolinsky — is weak-willed, with an artistic nature, and something of a mystic. He is a product of a different tradition, raised in Kiev by a Polish-Ukrainian father and a Russian mother. Dolinsky has separated from his shrewish wife after she has lured him into an unfortunate marriage. In Paris, where he is correspondent for a Russian newspaper, he meets two half-sisters, Dora and Anna. The three are most compatible, and on their return to Russia Dolinsky rents rooms in the large flat where they have a dressmaking business. Anna, a serious and noble woman, falls in love with Dolinsky, but loves him selflessly, from a distance. Dora, the more vivacious sister, falls ill with tuberculosis and must go to Nice for recovery. Since Anna cannot leave her business, Dolinsky accompanies her, initially as a nurse but eventually as her lover. Dora does not recover and Dolinsky is devastated by her death. He flees to Paris, where, under the influence of a devious Polish Jesuit, Father Zaionczek, he becomes a missionary in Paraguay. Anna never marries but lives on, cherishing her memories of Dolinsky.

Leskov attempts here to write a psychological novel, but fails to create an interesting and convincing hero. Dolinsky is a pale, limp character whose almost total passivity makes him ill-suited to be the central figure in a novel. (At least Oblomov, that other paragon of passivity, has a fascinating inner life.) But Dolinsky's history is simply a series of encounters in which he meekly follows the lead of other people: his wife traps him into marriage; Anna takes the initiative in declaring her love to him, as does Dora; a pair of *grisettes* attempts to seduce him in Paris; and finally Father Zaionczek pushes him into the Catholic Church. Leskov's attempts to convey the workings of Dolinsky's mind through lengthy inner monologues are muddled and unconvincing and never manage to clarify what his problems are.

The change of direction which Leskov followed to *The By-Passed* only led him to a dead end. His objections to the overwhelmingly civic concerns of the "progressive" novelists are certainly valid, but his own attempt to show a group of ordinary people coming to terms with purely personal problems is a clear failure.The intimate novel of the psychology of love in the manner of Turgenev was simply not Leskov's forte.

Leskov's third novel, *Ostrovitiane* (The Islanders, 1866), also very deliberately turns its back on the larger world of political and social questions. In his two earlier novels he suffered from a tendency to include too much material, burdening their plots with irrelevent, if often diverting, incidents and characters. He tries to avoid this failing in *The Islanders* by concentrating on just one family and attempting to create an idyll (his epigraph is from Theocritus). Leskov's attraction to this type of idealized family life already showed itself in the chapters of *The By-Passed* which dealt in highly sentimentalized fashion with the family of a French milkmaid, Gervaise (part 2, chapter 8). Here, however, he portrays a German family living on Vasily Island in St. Petersburg. The father, a craftsman, has died, leaving his widow, an aged mother, and two daughters, Ida and Maria, to carry on a small business. A third daughter is married to Friedrich Schultz, an ambitious and prosperous businessman. Maria (or Manya) is a thoughtful and sensitive girl, the idol of her family. On Manya's sixteenth birthday Schultz introduces her to Roman Istomin, a fashionable artist. Istomin is a notorious womanizer, and Manya soon falls in love with him. He seduces her, then tires of her and disappears, leaving her to bear his child. Schultz eventually takes Manya to Germany and arranges her marriage to a rich but misanthropic German. They live unhappily until Manya unexpectedly meets Istomin, who has been blinded and now makes a living as a pianist. Manya's husband, realizing that she feels no love for him, urges her to leave him and fulfill her ambition to become a writer. At the novel's end she is a successful author of a number of children's travel books. Istomin again disappears.

The form of the work — a first-person narrator relates the history of his friendship with the Nork family — is responsible for many of its failings. Such a technique is awkward for this type of story in any case, and Leskov does not carry it through consistently. Thus he must abandon the first-person narration in describing Manya's stay in Germany. Elsewhere he must strain the credulity of the reader to keep his narrator at the scene of the action. This involves some heavy traffic between the narrator's apartment and the Nork home, where he is summoned each time a family crisis occurs. Leskov also finds it necessary to have his narrator live in an apartment separated only by a curtain from Istomin's studio, thus allowing him to eavesdrop on several crucial occasions. The first-person "memoir" form which Leskov uses so effectively elsewhere simply does not work here in dealing with someone else's love story. Manya's relationship with Istomin is necessarily related from a distance; we have no inside views of her nor of Istomin, and are never close enough to either of them to become truly involved with their drama. Leskov often lapses into verbosity when describing the details of everyday life in his chosen milieu: the scene of Manya's birthday party, for example, runs on for thirty-seven pages.

Although Leskov is dealing with an insular world, he still manages to express his views on at least one contemporary issue. A dispute over esthetics had broken out in 1865 after the publication of the second edition of Chernyshevsky's essay, *The Aesthetic Relation of Art to Reality*. Leskov was apparently still in the process of working out his own views on art, and those sections of the novel dealing with the question appear unfinished. Thus his own views are never made absolutely clear, but he does heap scorn on both the anti-esthetic attitudes of nihilists and the sterility and lack of topicality of the Academy, implying that art must have a firm moral basis. He stresses that Manya had devoted herself to a kind of art which will be uplifting for children, whereas Istomin cultivates an amoral attitude, arguing for a pure art, free from any values save esthetic ones. Leskov suggests that Istomin carries this attitude over into his personal life, where his casual worship of Manya's beauty destroys the harmony of the Nork family. Istomin's views are not clearly stated, however, and the esthetic debate is poorly integrated into the fabric of the novel. But Leskov's ideas on art at this stage, however imperfectly they may be expressed, already anticipate those of Tolstoy.

Leskov's last completed conventional novel, *Na nozhakh* (At Daggers Drawn, 1870–71), bears all the marks of a potboiler and, indeed, was published at a time when he was in considerable financial difficulty. His main source of income was his newspaper feuilletons, which paid poorly and erratically, and thus the attraction of publishing a large, "sensational" work in Katkov's respected and well-paying *Russky vestnik* is understandable. It is a novel of intrigue whose calculated effects of mystery and horror, sudden climaxes, complex plot, and simply drawn characters place it in the tradition of the French *roman-feuilleton*. The main action is the attempt of Glafira Bodrostina, a beautiful and sensuous young woman, to dispose of her aged husband while yet ensuring that he will his money to her. She enlists the help of her former lover, Gordanov, a master of all forms of skulduggery. One of Gordonov's pawns is Iosaf Vislenev, an incredibly obtuse young man, easily manipulated into performing the meanest deeds provided he believes he is acting on the loftiest of motives. Extortion, arson, forgery, theft, and murder, together with numerous lesser crimes, fill the work's pages, while a tangle of love intrigues adds further complications.

At Daggers Drawn and *No Way Out* are often grouped with the "anti-nihilist" novels. To be sure, Gordanov was once part of the radical movement, and Vislenev writes for the radical press. But Leskov does not quarrel with the ideas of the nihilists directly; rather he wishes to show that the legacy of the materialism of the sixties is but cynical egoism. Gordanov, for instance, states that he acts on the basis of "Darwinism": "Swallow up the others or else they will swallow you up" (PSS, 23.90). This summarizes the ethical principles of most of the other characters as well. There are positive nihilists in the novel, although they play relatively minor roles. Anna Skokova — "a limited, dull, and zealous individual, and so quick that when she pronounced her first name, patronymic and surname, all that came from her lips was 'Vanskok' " (PSS, 23.137) — is selflessly dedicated to the cause.The other "honest nihilist" is Major Forov, a skeptic and atheist who, however, makes a point of keeping out of any party or group and who seems to be moving toward repentance at the time of his death. Thus the novel is not so much an attack on nihilism as a broad indictment of the cynical materialism of society as a whole.

Although the negative side is clearly at the center of the novel's stage, there is also a positive ideal, albeit only sketchily outlined. Podozerov, a young landowner whose sterling character Gordanov attempts to tarnish, expresses this liberal view: "I have no bias and am not the slave of any party; I respect and admire all sincere and honorable people on earth, provided that they desire the happiness of those near them and believe in what they say" (PSS, 24.93). Podozerov is a pale figure, however, who plays only a minor role in the action. A more convincing positive character is Father Evangel, "the poetic priest." Like Podozerov, Evangel is tolerant of those who disagree with him (his best friend is the nihilist Forov) and his ideal is quiet, rural family life. A small group of ordinary people living quietly in a provincial town is thus counterposed to the larger world of Petersburg, from whence come those who would disrupt that peaceful existence. But on the whole Leskov is much more fascinated by his negative characters. Thus the novel's main conflict is not one of good versus evil but of the villain's attempts to outwit one another.

More than any other work of Leskov's, *At Daggers Drawn* shows the influence of Dostoevsky.[6] Apart from complexity of intrigue, Leskov uses Dostoevskian techniques of composition such as the "conclave" (Leonid Grossman's term), in which characters are periodically gathered together to play out a strikingly melodramatic scene. Leskov also tries, with less success, to create some Dostoevskian characters. Glafira Bodrostina resembles Nastasya Fillipovna in *The Idiot*: she too was seduced and abandoned at an early age, and her conduct thereafter is motivated by her desire for revenge for past humiliations alternating with periods of self-hate and remorse. She too is a proud and sensual woman who delights in humiliating her many admirers (she even carries a whip!). Larisa Visleneva, Iosaf's sister, is, like Aglaya Epanchina, a pure-hearted young woman desperately seeking someone worthy of her love. The description of the investigation of Bodrostin's murder contains pages reminiscent of *Crime and Punishment*. But the characters lack the depth and subtlety of Dostoevsky's creations, and Leskov's attempts to convey their inner lives are unsteady, confusing rather than suggestive. Too often he is forced to suspend the story and explain motivations rather than demonstrate them through the actions of his characters.

Apart from these flaws, the novel is full of cheap effects included solely in an attempt to develop and sustain a sense of mystery but with little relevance to the plot. Thus there are a number of hints at supernatural happenings, prophecies of a half-mad landowner as well as those of a mysterious deaf-mute girl, and several visions. Leskov simply loses his sense of proportion in his eagerness to tell an exciting story.

Leskov's early novels deal with fairly conventional literary characters (Dolinsky, the aimless, self-doubting hero; Istomin, the bored and cynical seducer; Manya and Anna, the pure, strong-willed heroines) who act out fairly conventional literary situations (the triangular love conflict). *No Way Out*, the best of the four novels, is an exception: the measure of freshness which Leskov achieves here is largely due to his reliance on his own experience and his immediate response to the events of the day with minimal regard for literary prototypes. But his efforts at writing a conventional novel did little to win him his own place in Russian literature. He himself complained that the novelistic conventions of his day were too cramping and was fond of quoting the formula "fell in love — got married; fell in love — shot himself" (*vliubilsia-zhenilsia*; *vliubilsia-zastrelilsia*) to sum up the range of standard plots.[7] The narrator of *Detskie gody* (Childhood Years, 1874) best expresses Leskov's changed views on the novel:

I shall relate all this not in the manner in which things are told in novels — and this, I believe, may constitute a certain interest, perhaps even a novelty and may even provide some edification. I shall not abbreviate some incidents nor inflate the significance of others. I shall not be compelled to do this by the artificial and unnatural form of the novel, which demands a rounding off of the plot and the concentration of everything around one center. Things do not happen this way in life. The life of a man runs on like a scroll unwinding from a spool and so I shall simply unroll it like a ribbon in the notes which I offer here. (5.279)

The unifying center of the later works thus shifts from the plot to the narrator, often a highly individualized figure whose speech traits assume new importance (*skaz*). The narrator relates events in a more or less chronological sequence using a loose, episodic structure in which small events may be given as much attention as larger ones. Diverse material and lengthy disgressions are included, and the anecdote becomes the basic building block of the structure. The central love story with its psychological underpinnings is minimized or totally abandoned. The result is a loosely constructed work, full of incident and closer in form to the eighteenth-century English novel of Fielding and Sterne than to its nineteenth-century counterpart. A form which can admit all of the above qualities — the memoir — becomes dominant in Leskov's longer prose narratives. As he wrote to Fedor Buslaev: "[The memoir form] seems very convenient for me: there is more life in it or, to put it better, it is more genuine than the depiction through scenes in which, when arranged together even by such masters as Walter Scott, there appears such an obvious strain or, as the common people say, 'Things happen just as in a novel' " (10.452).

II   Cathedral Folk

The first work to reflect these ideas, at least in part, is *Cathedral Folk*. Leskov worked on the novel for six years, and its history of publication is complex. The title of the first version, *Waiting for the Moving of the Water,* refers to the Biblical story of the sick who waited for the miraculous healing which occurred when an angel troubled the waters of the pool of Siloam. Even at this stage Leskov was insistent about the peculiar genre of the work, and wrote his editor: "In your announcement in the next issue I earnestly implore you . . . to write not 'a major work of fiction' but to state frankly 'a novelistic chronicle' . . . for it will be a chronicle and not a novel. Thus it was conceived and thus it grows by the grace of God. We are not much accustomed to such a thing, but we shall learn" (10.260).

The work was first intended as a large-scale history of a provincial town, in which the clergy were but one element among many townsfolk of all social levels who were to be portrayed. Several plot lines began to emerge before Leskov suspended publication after three installments in 1867 because of editors' cuts which he found intolerable. In January 1868, he renewed publication of a revised version entitled *Bozhedomy* (Dwellers in the House of God) in *Literaturnaya biblioteka* (Literary Library). Only two installments had appeared when the journal unexpectedly closed. This second version is much closer to *Cathedral Folk* in that its focus is narrowed to the clergy. Extraneous material was meanwhile published independently ("Kotin the Provider," "The Plodomasov Dwarfs" "Old Times in Plodomasovo"). It was not until 1872, after further disputes with editors which led to a court case, that the work finally appeared in Katkov's *Russky vestnik* under its present title.

Leskov described his work as follows: "Its heroes are somewhat unusual — they are the clergy of an ideal Russian town. The plot of the novel, or to put it better, of the 'history', is the struggle of the best of these characters with those who would sabotage Russia's development" (10.279). Leading the struggle is the archpriest of Stargorod, Savely Tuberozov, a sensible and upright man in his seventies whose air of dignity is created not only by his majestic, leonine hair but also by his unshakable conviction of the rightness of his cause. His reading of the scriptures and church history convinces him that "Christianity has still not been preached in Russia" (4.59), and he devotes himself to instilling a basic, practical Christianity in his congregation and to bringing the church closer to the real needs of the people. This sets him at odds with the church's own ossified bureaucracy, which even at the very beginning of his career discourages him from relating his sermons to real life. We learn of Tuberozov's conflicts with ecclesiastical and civil authorities from his diary, a remarkable chronicle of his thirty-five years as a priest.

A more specific opponent to Tuberozov appears in Termosesov, an ex-nihilist now striving to make a career for himself in the civil service. Termosesov (and by implication the government bureaucracy as a whole) fears an independent clergy, and he begins plotting to ruin the archpriest. "As soon as faith becomes a serious faith," he says, "then it is unhealthy and must be narrowed down and restricted" (4.173). Tuberozov is aware of Termosesov's schemes and realizes that his end is near. After a mystical experience in a thunderstorm he decides he must preach one final, eloquent sermon affirming the need for ideals and faith and stressing tradition as a basis for living. He castigates those whom he has summoned to the church for the insincerity of their religion and speaks of creating a new church in the desert. Termosesov takes careful note and denounces Tuberozov, who is removed from his post and dies, defeated and embittered.

Leskov attached great importance to the positive characters in the work, particularly to Tuberozov as an example of a genuinely good man. He describes him as "a man of integrity, strong, poetic, and at the same time filled with civic spirit; a man of intellect and tender love with an ideal and living faith. In creating him I felt that I had the great happiness to do something which could raise man higher than matters of the flesh and self-interest."[8] Yet Tuberozov has enough human qualities to make him credible. The episode of the three canes presented to the Stargorod clergy which drew him into a squabble over the privileges of rank reveals a certain pettiness in his nature. In spite of his tolerance of the Old Believers, he is narrow-minded and extremely conservative, as his diary entries show. He is, after all, the product of a typical ecclesiastical education and has spent most of his life in sleepy Stargorod, where trifles assume enormous significance.

The life in the book comes from Deacon Akhilla, one of Leskov's most memorable creations, a man of immense physical strength and the soul of a child. The disparity between his behaviour (wearing spurs under his vestments; winning a wrestling match with a touring performer) and the restrained habits expected from a man of the cloth is a constant source of comedy. Akhilla's character reflects Tuberozov's, but on a different level. Just as Akhilla's humanity is too great to be contained within his role in the church and constantly spills over, so Tuberozov's religious faith cannot find expression within the narrow limits prescribed by his official role. Both came to grief because of an excess of something within them.

The plot takes the form of a jumble of loosely connected anecdotes. We must remember that Leskov insisted he was writing not a conventional novel with a tightly knit plot but a chronicle where trifles and peripheral incidents may be placed on the same level as matters of great import. But a closer examination will also show the plot is not as loose as it first appears, and that the trifling incidents, when taken together, do move toward a conclusion.[9] Thus Akhilla finds himself in disgrace after the cane incident which opens the book, and in order to regain favor with Tuberozov he begins combating the "heresies" of Varnava Prepotensky, a nihilist schoolteacher, all the more energetically. He makes an enemy of Varnava, who is happy to get his revenge on the local clergy by helping Termosesov. Varnava inspires "heresies" in Danilka, a local factotum, until Akhilla is provoked into assaulting him. This provides Termosesov with a pretext to force Danilka to write a complaint reflecting on the Stargorod clergy as a whole. Likewise, the episode of the Plodomasov dwarfs seems a totally independent tale within the work and was, in fact, published independently. But it does have a purpose here: Nikolay Afanasevich's story of how the strong-willed but good-hearted Plodomasova acquired him and took pity on him enraptures Tuberozov, who cites it as an example of the "old tradition" (*staraia skazka*) which he fears is disappearing. The dwarf's tale does nothing to advance the plot, but Leskov's point is that even under serfdom — a system which he clearly abhorred — there existed the possibility of loving human relationships. It was this attitude — "tender-hearted Russia," Tuberozov calls it, or the capacity to maintain a truly human relationship in an inhuman system — that led Tuberozov to cite the story as an example of the healthy legacy from the past whose spirit he tries to keep alive. Termosesov's arrival immediately after the dwarf's story is thus of some import, for it is he who seeks to destroy this old tradition. Another genre scene, a portrait of townsfolk bathing in the river early in the morning, also does nothing to advance the plot but contributes to the picture of an idealized, harmonious world ("an ideal Russian town") in which relations between townspeople are as loving and easy as those within a happy family.

Leskov does poke fun at the neatly organized plots of more conventional novels. Thus much of the work is taken up by farcical battle between Deacon Akhilla and the nihilistic schoolteacher Varnava Prepotensky. Varnava, determined to study man from a purely materialistic point of view, has acquired the skeleton of a drowned man; Akhilla, outraged at such sacrilege, is equally determined to give the bones a Christian burial. Their encounters allow Leskov to indulge in a good deal of Sternian play with the idea of the plot. Leskov creates a false sense of drama and suspense by frequent asides to the reader stressing the import of the battle of the bones and postponing the fateful confrontation between Varnava and Akhilla: "And thus, at last, the hour has struck when Varnava's retribution by the hand of Akhilla is to begin, and when the great Stargorod drama, which absolutely coincides with this event, a drama which makes up the subject of our chronicle, is to begin" (4.23). In fact the "great Stargorod drama" never comes off; the bones are thrown away and Varnava leaves town.

Hugh McLean has rightly pointed out a major weakness in *Cathedral Folk* in Leskov's failure to analyze the reasons for the decline of faith and to present any serious struggle between faith and unbelief.[10] Leskov's own description of the work as Tuberozov's "struggle against saboteurs" perhaps applies to a book he may have intended to write but never achieved. What we see of Tuberozov's struggle has little intensity and hardly moves the plot. He scarcely confronts Termosesov, and once the denunciation is sent his fate is sealed. Akhilla's "defense of the faith" serves as a farcical counterpoint to Tuberozov's and often overshadows it, detracting from any serious purpose Leskov may have had in mind. Leskov is curiously reluctant to portray any direct confrontation between Tuberozov and "the enemies of Russia's development." His final sermon, which one would expect to be an inspired climax to the book (it is Tuberozov's last chance to state his case) is a disappointment: we learn only fragments of what he says, pieced together from his notes. The diary which chronicles his earlier conflicts is itself a device which distances the reader from the action, for its entries record a gradual erosion of Savely's earlier passionate devotion to his cause. Its last words are particularly significant: "I have become shallower and shallower in every way ... No, once I was not like that, I was not enticed by such trifles. I was engrossed in lofty thoughts so that having perfected myself in this earthly vale of tears, I might see the light which knoweth no setting and return tenfold the talents entrusted to me by the Lord" (4.81). Tuberozov fails in his life's work, and there is little indication that much remains of his spirit in Stargorod. After a brief but futile rebellion he dies, leaving no progeny.

The diverse elements which enter into the work — the farcical adventures of Akhilla, nihilist skulduggery, the dignified but pathetic end to Tuberozov's career, a wistful evocation of an obsolescent way of life — produce a mixed impression because they are not welded together by a single purpose. Ostensibly, Leskov's purpose is to defend the church, but the lack of conviction with which he does so makes it a shaky defense indeed. *Cathedral Folk* provides additional evidence that Leskov's views on religion were already changing and that the rift between him and the church was growing wider. It is not surprising that in later life he rejected what he called the "idealized Byzantinism"[11] with which he portrayed Tuberozov. His repudiation of the work was based on ideological rather than esthetic grounds, and the book certainly has little impact as a defense of religion. Its undeniable appeal stems rather from its warm portrayal of a distant and distinctive way of life and its vivid characters, Tuberozov and Akhilla.

III   *Other Chronicles*

While Leskov was working on the early versions of *Cathedral Folk* he conceived the idea of another ambitious work, a trilogy dealing with three generations of a single family, the Plodomasovs. S. S. Dudyshkin, editor of *Otechestvennye zapiski,* enthusiastically supported the project, but these plans were disrupted by Dudyshkin's unexpected death in 1866. The trilogy was abandoned, but Leskov used portions of it in *Cathedral Folk,* and in 1869 published three sketches dealing with the Boyarina Plodomasova.

Leskov's turn to a large-scale historical subject was in keeping with the spirit of the times. Like Tolstoy, he was attempting to reassess Russian life after the turmoil of the reform period of the 1860s, to determine what Russianness meant, and, in a period when established norms were being questioned or discredited, to set forth a more permanent set of ethical values in his fiction. But Leskov's approach to history is very diffierent from Tolstoy's; he was not a deep thinker and was not attempting to create any original theory of history. As he said, "I greatly appreciate and love this science [history] but I can serve only one aspect of it, the light and superficial aspect, the aspect of portraying certain unimportant people who, however, by their very lives express to a certain extent the history of their time" (7.522). His concern, then, is to create memorable and representative characters rather than to reproduce the minutiae of life in the past.

Although the three Plodomasova sketches are very much centered on character, they still have exciting, even melodramatic plots. Their flavor is reminiscent of Sir Walter Scott's novels or of Pushkin's *The Captain's Daughter*. The first sketch, set in 1748, relates how the Boyar Nikita Plodomasov, a tyrannical and profligate landowner, carries off the daughter of a neighboring landowner after she has refused his proposal of marriage. He is fifty-one, his intended, Marfa, fifteen. But Marfa turns out to have more spirit than Nikita bargained for and quickly tames his wild nature. The second sketch, set some thirty-five years later, describes the now widowed Marfa Plodomasova. One of her maids becomes pregnant by her son; she is furious and has him beaten (to which the son humbly, almost eagerly submits), then lavishes care on her maid. A band of brigands, "inspired by the success of Pugachev's uprising,"[12] breaks into the house and tortures Marfa to force her to hand over her valuables. She resists courageously until she is saved by a minor miracle. Her maid dies giving birth to a son (the future Tuganov, who figures briefly in *Cathedral Folk*). In both sketches the denouement is brought about by convenient coincidence. In the first, Marfa is about to jump out of the window and kill herself to avoid marriage when she is saved by troops sent to arrest Nikita; in the second, a sudden gust of wind seems to come as the answer to Marfa's prayers and alarms the bandits who are about to murder her. The third sketch is set in a much later era, after Plodomasova's death, and appears in essentially the same form in the dwarf's tale in *Cathedral Folk*.

The dominant figure in the sketches is Marfa Plodomasova, a strong-willed, even tyrannical woman who, however, is stubbornly committed to a set of high principles. Leskov engages in some social criticism here, for it was precisely this firm devotion to principle which he found lacking in contemporary society. Marfa is vividly drawn but fails to convince fully because we never understand what motivates her. Leskov makes her and the other characters change radically and abruptly but provides little explanation for their behavior. Marfa, when first kidnapped by Nikita, is adamant in refusing to marry him; he forces a priest to conduct the ceremony but when soldiers break into the house to arrest him he is overcome by a sudden onrush of guilt for his past sins. This crisis is partly motivated by what he thinks is a vision — a typical Leskovian device for conveying deep psychological processes. Marfa in turn forgives him with equal abruptness and accepts the marriage, after which Nikita's willful character is totally reformed. Marfa's character in the second sketch suffers from the same lack of consistency. Leskov is almost as fond of portraying extremes in his characters as is Dostoevsky, but unlike the latter he fails to provide the reader with the insights into his creations which would make their behavior convincing. In spite of this, however, he does manage to reproduce in Marfa Plodomasova the blend of piety and patriarchal harshness which marked the manners of the eighteenth-century landowners.

The idea of a trilogy involving several generations of a single family recurred in *Zakhudalyi rod* (A Family in Decline), which once again was left unfinished because of problems of publication. Three installments appeared in Katkov's *Russky vestnik*, but the editor's arbitrary changes in the text infuriated Leskov and precipitated his break with Katkov. Leskov complained that the affair had sapped his will to complete the novel as originally planned, and so contented himself with restoring the passages deleted from the "Katkov version" for a separate edition of 1875. In 1889, while preparing his *Collected Works*, Leskov added a concluding chapter and made a number of other revisions which stressed Tolstoyan ideas. Yet the work does end as Leskov originally planned, and it may be considered finished, if not on such an ambitious scale as originally intended.

A Family in Decline is written more deliberately in the form of a chronicle, with both real and imagined events arranged roughly in time sequence (although there are flashbacks) and both historical and fictional personages as actors. There is only a meager plot line; Leskov once again concentrates on creating a series of highly colorful and original figures. His aim, like that of the original old Russian chroniclers, is to preserve something of the past for posterity: not necessarily its day-to-day facts, but what the chronicler decided

was worthy of preservation. Although his subject is the family itself, the center of the work is the Princess Varvara Nikanorovna
Protozanova, an upright, strong-willed, independent woman in
whom charity and tolerance coexist with stubbornness and stern-
ness. The chronicler of the family is the princess's granddaughter,
who recalls "what her memory has preserved" (5.9) and what other
members of the household have told her. Her narrative flows at a
leisurely pace, pausing when she finds a pretext to relate an interesting anecdote or describe an eccentric character.

The division of her narrative into two books has its logic: the
first presents a picture of the past, the positive ideal exemplified in
the way of life of the princess and her relationship to those around
her. Her friends are themselves by no means aristocrats, but "the
bypassed," virtuous people whose claim to nobility lies in their
moral worth rather than their lineage. This portrait of the "old
legend" ends ominously: "But there, beyond the walls of the
house, rolled and thundered another sort of life, new and cut off
from its own home-grown traditions: there was a different sort of
people on whom the country looked in astonishment as a hen looks
when she finds she has hatched ducklings" (5.114).

The second book contains the essential plot of the work: this
takes place in the first two decades of the nineteenth century and
treats the actual decline of the Protozanov family. This is presented
as a gradual alienation of the princess from her society caused by
society's evolution away from the ideals of the princess. Religion is
one of the main factors which isolates the princess from her peers.
She insists on putting her beliefs into practice and is hardly attuned
to the new religious currents of the day, rationalism and mysticism.
She is disgusted that a distant relative, Princess Khotetova, should
devote her wealth to the building of chapels while her peasants
starve. The princess's views on the aristocracy also do little to en-
dear her to her peers: she insists that one's deeds are of greater importance than one's name, and belittles the role of the aristocracy
in the war against Napoleon and its probable role in the eventual
emancipation of the serfs. Her peers spread malicious gossip about
her and she is eventually ostracized. The isolation of the princess
from her age is increased when she reluctantly sends her daughter
to be educated at a fashionable institute in St. Petersburg. Here the
girl is given a set of values quite alien to the family tradition, and so
further estranged from her mother.

The final stage in the decline of the princess's fortunes occurs with the appearance of Count Funkendorf, a Baltic German (a type for which Leskov reserved special scorn). Just as in *Cathedral Folk*, an alien force from St. Petersburg intrudes to disrupt a harmonious way of life. After the princess rejects the Count's proposal of marriage, he turns his attentions to her daughter and, aided by the intrigues of Princess Khotetova, is successful. The daughter's lavish dowry includes most of the Protozanov estates, and the Count as new owner proceeds to resettle the peasants. The princess accepts financial ruin by sacrificing the remainder of her fortune to save them.

Among the princess's entourage are some highly idealized positive figures: her devoted servant Patrikey, her maid Olga, who sacrifices her love for a seminarian to allow him to make a career in the church, and some overdrawn eccentrics. Chief among the latter is Rogozhin, an impoverished aristocrat who sees himself as a Don Quixote determined to fight injustice and defend the rights of the weak. Rogozhin is also a defender of the aristocracy, not only in its narrow class definition but in the broader sense of all those possessing genuine nobility of spirit. It is largely through Rogozhin's remarks that Leskov conveys his idea of the growing spiritual impoverishment of society. Rogozhin has a fixation on trinities, one of which he sees as the basis of Russia: tsar, aristocracy, and people. The tsar is the head, the people the stomach, and the aristocracy the heart of the nation. It is the heart, the spirit of nobility, which he sees as bankrupt.

A second eccentric plays a smaller but still important role in the work as a mouthpiece for Tolstoyan teachings. This is Chervev, a former professor whose unorthodox views lead to his expulsion from the seminary where he had taught. Rogozhin voices ultimate praise for him as one who has "comprehended the way, the truth, life" (5.161). Zhuravsky, a respected friend of the princess and a historical figure, recommends Chervev as a "genuine Christian" who would be a remarkable tutor for the princess's sons if she wishes to raise them to become neither officers nor courtiers but people. Speaking with Chervev, she learns of his total commitment to nonviolence, his unalterable (if nonviolent) opposition to conventional ethics, the official church, and the existing social order. She realizes that if he educates her sons, they can only look forward to a life of isolation and persecution because of their ideals. She cannot summon the courage to commit her sons to such a life, and so dismisses him. But the encounter stirs her to reexamine her own beliefs and implicitly to an awareness of the failings of Christianity as preached by the church. Chervev ends his days as an exile in the North, the princess's sons are forced into an education "in keeping with their noble lineage," while the princess lives modestly and repentantly on her estate, supported by her sons.

Princess Protozanova's character and her history have much in common with those of Tuberozov. Both are firmly rooted in an older tradition; both are highly respected by their immediate circles but alienated from the larger life around them; both are, at the end of their days, shaken into an awareness that the previous basis of their religion was inadequate; both end defeated by new forces hostile to their way of life. Both works lament the end of an era: Tuberozov dies without progeny; the princess has been unable to keep alive the values of the true aristocracy in her children. But just as in *Cathedral Folk*, there is little drama in the conflict between the old and new forces, and little analysis of the reasons for the decline of nobility of the spirit. Leskov does point out the growth of the acquisitive spirit among the educated classes, but does not show why the positive ideal set out in the first portion of the work, even when championed by such stalwarts as Princess Protozanova, fails to withstand the onslaught of something portrayed as much less attractive and much weaker. In general the work does not warrant the extravagantly high praise Leskov lavished on it some fifteen years after the writing. Its positive figures are too virtuous to be credible, its eccentrics overdrawn or sentimentalized, its villains too hypocritical to play the role of convincing opponents. The Tolstoyan-inspired ending is too forced, and its artificial nature cannot be camouflaged, The work's chief success is the figure of the princess herself, whose language, forthright manner, and strength of character all ring true.

Another novel-length work, unfinished but complete in itself, was written in 1874 and published the following year in the journal *Niva* under the title *Bluzhdaiushchie ogon'ki* (Will-o-the-Wisps: Praottsev's Autobiography). In a separate edition of 1876, Leskov restored some passages previously cut by the censor and changed title to *Detskie gody* (Childhood Years). The work is also in memoir form, but unlike *A Family in Decline*, the subject is the memoirist's own life. A fragment from an unpublished foreword (5.605–8) explains the "origins" of the work. The narrator of this foreword, while spending the summer in a quiet provincial town, meets a local monk, Father Gordy, a man of striking appearance, a brilliant cel-

list, and an artist of considerable talent. Speculation naturally
arises about how such a man found his way to an isolated monastery in a provincial backwater. The foreword breaks off at this
point and we must assume that the narrating "I" has acquired and
published Father Gordy's autobiography after his death.

The autobiographer, Merkul Praottsev, thus sets out to tell his
life's story and to explain how he came to be Father Gordy. He
writes as an old man, surveying the errors and failings of his youth
with total candor, viewing them as "will-o-the-wisps" whose
momentary brightness only led him astray from his destined path to
the monastery. His first memory provides an illustration: he recalls
his parent's horror when they returned home to find him clinging to
the outside of the window frame, five stories above the street. His
father, a choleric and tyrannical cavalry officer, rescues him, and is
convinced that his son has seen a vision which he followed and tried
to capture. Merkul himself vaguely remembers "something light
and delicate and beautiful . . . which seemed to be drawing me after
it" (5.283). The vararies of Merkul's pursuit of this vision make up
the content of his autobiography. After his father's death, Merkul
is sent to the St. Petersburg Cadet Corps for military education. A
"mutiny" in the Cadet Corps causes his expulsion and he, together
with seven others, is sent home. The account of their month-long
journey from St. Petersburg to Kiev is a miniature epic in itself, full
of curious and absorbing incident. It is on this journey that Merkul
experiences the first pleasures and pains of freedom which lead him
to an awareness of his own individuality. But the accidental drowning of one of their company leads him to a crisis: as he draws closer
to Kiev and the encounter with his mother, whom he idealizes as the
personification of goodness, he is overwhelmed with guilt for his
past actions on the journey. His freedom now becomes a burden,
and he decides the only way to rid himself of it is to withdraw into a
monastery. A fine comic scene ensues between Merkul and a Greek
monk — an episodic character most vividly sketched. Merkul's ardent confession of his past and his pleas to be allowed to lead a life
of asceticism are heard by the monk, who presses on him coffee,
rum, wine, and other delicacies, while a "rosy woman" listens with
great interest as she munches Turkish delight. The monk advises
him first to experience life, gesturing toward the wine and the
woman, and then tells of his own exploits with a maximum of exuberance and a minimum of grammar.

Merkul finds the guidance he has sought when he arrives in Kiev.

He scarcely crosses the threshold before his mother, Katerina Vasilevna, outlines a demanding program of instruction in which every
hour of the day has its assigned purpose. She is of Baltic German
stock and is determined to give her son an education which would
"ennoble the feelings and enlighten the mind and heart" (5.335).
His mother's influence is gradually undermined by the man whom
she engages to teach her son mathematics, Professor Altansky. He
is a serene and humane man, more concerned with imparting wis-
dom than with following the mother's program, who awakens a
genuine thirst for knowledge in Merkul. A second factor leads
much more directly to his disillusionment with his mother's approach to life. Professor Altansky's daughter, Khristya, is in love
with a ne'er-do-well, Serge, whose family opposed the marriage.
Katerina Vasilevna convinces Khristya that the only proper course
is to reject Serge, which she does. He marries unhappily, but Khristya, still devoted to him, then decides that their personal happiness
is more important than conventional morality and becomes his mistress. She dies giving birth to his child and Merkul realizes that his
mother bears much of the responsibility for the unhappy situation.
Only later does Merkul discover that his mother's life contained a
drama like Khristya's: she rejected the love of a German artist,
Phillip Kolberg, in order to devote herself totally to her son's education. Katerina Vasilevna, aware that she has demanded too much
of Khristya and of her son, as well as of herself, ends by taking her
own life.

It is only when freed from his mother's influence that Merkul begins to be aware of his real talents and inclinations. He meets an
artist, Laptev, and experiences with him the thrill of creativity.
Laptev recognizes Merkul's talents but does not readily encourage
him to an artistic career; indeed, he warns him of the sacrifices and
total dedication which such a life will demand of him. But Merkul
accepts this and goes to study with Kolberg. Kolberg, portrayed
only sketchily as an extraordinarily wise and highly idealized
figure, was presumably intended to play a large role in the succeed-
ing parts, which remained unwritten.

Merkul's development, then, had moved through a series of
stages: the discipline and restrictions of his early family life and the
Cadet Corps; the total freedom of his journey to Kiev; the renewed
discipline of his mother's regime; Altansky's approach, which
stresses self-discovery; and the ending, when he is once again freed
to start afresh. The ideal toward which Merkul seems to be striving

is that of a harmonious nature which combines, as in so many of Leskov's positive figures, the sensitivity and creativity of the artist with basic Christian ethics. We know little of Merkul's religious feelings apart from his conventional Orthodox upbringing — his mother, born a Lutheran, converted to Orthodoxy — and his dim awareness, resulting from Altansky's conversations, that the religious beliefs of his society were far from true Christianity, an ideal to which one can strive only by "rowing against a stiff current of egotistical, base passions" (5.400). Merkul thus has far to go before we can fully understand how he came to the monastery, and his further spiritual development in life was presumably to be the major topic of later parts.

It is ironic that on this occasion, when Leskov took pains to warn his readers that he was not writing in the usual "artificial and unnatural form of the novel" (5.279), he in fact produced a remarkably well-knit narrative. The diffuseness and abundance of extraneous incident of most of his earlier novels are absent here; the parts fit nicely together to form a *Bildungsroman*. Despite its coherent plot, some finely drawn characters, and some well-planned scenes, the work is not free from typical Leskovian flaws. His style occasionally becomes overly sentimental, especially when he treats Khristya's love affair. The character of Kolberg remains highly abstract and idealized. Katerina Vasilevna's suicide occurs all too abruptly, and seems quite out of keeping with her sober and saintly character.

The question of why Leskov never completed the work must, in the absence of any factual evidence, remain a matter of speculation. But several hypotheses may be suggested. Given his current disillusionment with the official church, it seems difficult to imagine how he could create a positive hero whose final purpose in life was to live an ideal existence within the walls of a monastery. If the enlightened Father Gordy did so, he would probably express opinions about the church which would make the work impossible to publish. The circumstances of Leskov's life at the time perhaps also influenced his decision not to continue the work. He had broken with Katkov and was in a period of thorough-going self-examination. Considering his disillusionment with literature, so complete that he was seeking other employment at the time, it is surprising that the work so strongly affirms art as a calling. Perhaps the novel had a much more personal, "therapeutic" function for Leskov: in exploring Merkul's formative years and his decision to dedi-

cate himself to an artistic career, Leskov reaffirmed his own commitment to art.

Two final unfinished novels give evidence of Leskov's still unful-
filled desire to create a large social novel surveying the period from
the sixties to the eighties.[13] Only twelve short chapters of *Sokolii
perelet* (The Falcon's Flight) were published[14] in 1883 before Leskov abandoned it after his dismissal from the Ministry of Education. As he explained in an open letter, he had begun the novel
several years earlier, when conditions for publishing were much
freer: "I wanted to portray in the novel the 'falcon's flight' from
the ideas which I described twenty years ago in the novel *No Way
Out* to the ideas of the present time. Many of the characters whom
my readers know from *No Way Out* were to reappear in *The Falcon's Flight*. ...But I know very well that it would not be very
agreeable to the present view of literature.... I am stopping publication simply because, correctly or incorrectly, I find this time
quite inappropriate for a *social novel*, written truthfully as I at least
would try to write it, without submitting to party or other pressure."[15] No doubt the novel would have raised a storm had it
passed the censorship — which tightened considerably in the 1880s
— since Leskov tackles a delicate subject. The existing fragment is
set in 1863 and concerns a prison warden, Kolybelnikov, who
manages to rehabilitate his prisoners with a minimum of harshness
through compassion and respect for their dignity. The prison is to
be expanded to hold political prisoners, and the authorities decide
that Kolybelnikov's methods will no longer be suitable. It appears
that the main conflict in the novel was to be between the conventional morality and the Tolstoyan Christianity which Kolybelnikov
represents.

Nezametnyi sled (Inconspicuous Footprints) appeared in the following year[16] and likewise was never completed. It treats many of
the same themes as *The Falcon's Flight* but transfers them to an
earlier age — the 1830s and 1840s — when they could be handled
with less likelihood of provoking the censor. The novel's links with
The Falcon's Flight are direct, since it treats the childhood of
Adam Bezbedovich who is mentioned in the former novel as the
tutor of Kolybelnikov's daughter. But the action of the published
portions concentrates on the life of Adam's father, an idealized
version of Leskov's own father. The elder Bezbedovich is a righteous man whose stubborn refusal to bear false testimony leads to
the financial ruin of his family. He dies of cholera in 1842, embit-

tered and broken, leaving two sons (the elder, Adam, born in 1831, like Leskov) to be educated by the family's only friend, the local deacon. The novel was intended as another "family chronicle" narrated by the second son of Bezbedovich. Adam would presumably grow up as a high-minded "man without tendency" (a term hostile neighbors applied to the elder Bezbedovich) whose conscience brings him into conflict with the existing order.

Leskov's career as a novelist thus shows an evolution away from the more conventional genre of his time — a work which typically centered on a love story and treated the psychology of the protagonists in fine detail while showing the development of character — toward a looser structure in which the personality of the narrator rather than a tightly integrated plot provides the unifying center. In his remarks on the novel and his reluctance to be constrained by the "fell in love, got married — fell in love, shot himself" formula, Leskov argues that man's life is not exhausted by the larger events of love and death. Indeed, most of it is made up of "trifles" which may be as revealing of character as a major crisis. Thus he uses a form which is flexible enough to include such small events. In place of the gradual unfolding of a single personality which may sustain interest in a more conventional novel, Leskov includes many characters and many colorful events.

Leskov's own approach to the writing of a novel is also revealing. He conceives only a broad framework, then proceeds to create individual characters and events which he fits into the structure in the fashion of a mosaic. He did not believe in writing his novels according to a prearranged plan, he told an interviewer shortly before his death.[17] Thus material from one novel is often easily transferred to another or detached to form an independent work. The danger in such an approach — one which Leskov did not always avoid — is the "tendency to include too much" which he spoke of early in his career, resulting in a work which lacks unity. Indeed, it seems that most of Leskov's novels are themselves but fragments of a single large work which, like Dostoevsky's *Life of a Great Sinner,* he planned for many years but never managed to achieve. Leskov's unwritten novel could best be called *Notes of a Man Without Tendency*, and even at the end of his life he referred to plans for a work so entitled.

The major concern of Leskov's novels is an attempt at analyzing the ethical basis of society. The sixties had changed this basis radically, and Leskov's novels take a highly critical view of the new standards. Yet Leskov, at least before his Tolstoyan phase, failed to supply any very convincing alternative. The old prereform and, indeed, essentially pre-Petrine way of life is held up rather wistfully, not so much as an alternative but as a means of criticizine his own age.

This paucity of ideas in Leskov's novels seems one reason why he failed to complete so many of them. To be sure, he suffered more than most writers from harassment by the censors and from disputes with editors which caused him to curtail publication, yet he seems to have been aware that his novels lacked something, an awareness that led him to abandon them when he encountered an obstacle. "When the novelist undertakes to weave the fabric of his novel," Leskov wrote, "he must also be a thinker, he must show the living creatures of his fantasy in their relationship to a given time, environment, and to the state of science, art, and, very often, politics" (10.450). Leskov's talents simply did not run in this direction. Nor was Leskov a psychologist in the same sense as his novelist contemporaries were. For depth of psychological analysis he substitutes breadth, in the sense of creating highly eccentric, unusual characters, whose lives are so full of external color and interest that we almost forget how little we know of their inner lives. At his best, he creates some brilliant and memorable portraits; at worst, overdrawn, improbable caricatures. Leskov's gifts were those of a storyteller and an *ocherkist* — an imaginative journalist with a keen eye for detail, a sharp ear for the nuances of the spoken language, and a marvelously creative memory. The anecdote and the *ocherk* may be fitted into the loose framework Leskov devised, but taken together his novels cannot rival the brilliant creations of his contemporaries. Yet in letters from the last years of his life he frequently mentions titles of new novels planned or begun — *Ubezhishche* (The Refuge), *Bezbedovich*, *Eretik Fornosov* (Fornosov the Heretic). The novel was still the principal means of making a statement in art, and Leskov had much he wished to say.

CHAPTER 4

Stories and Tales

I Three Masterpieces

ALTHOUGH Leskov did not abandon the novel in the 1870s, the emphasis in his work shifted to shorter genres which were more in harmony with his talents.

Two subjects close to his heart provided the stimulus for one of his finest stories, "Zapechatlennyi angel" (The Sealed Angel, 1873). He had been interested in the Old Believers since childhood, and his 1863 study of the question of separate schools for them proved that he had become something of an authority on their way of life. A series of newspaper and journal articles devoted to the Old Believers reveals that, although he admired their independence and tenacity in defending their faith and supported their right to preserve it, he did not in the least romanticize them. Their narrow faith based on the dead letter of their canonical literature led him to conclude that they could have little positive influence on Russian religious life. But he was fascinated by their anachronistic way of life, a living link with the past. In particular, the Old Believer's resistance to change had enabled them to preserve the traditional style of icon-painting free from later influences.

The art of icon-painting, and religious art in general, was another subject which had captured Leskov's attention from his youth. While in Orel he followed with interest the painting of the iconostasis in the Church of St. Nikita; the eleventh-century frescoes in the St. Sofia Cathedral were being restored during his stay in Kiev. Leskov read several contemporary studies of icon-painting and joined the author of one, Fedor Buslaev, in lamenting the loss of the genuine native tradition as Western influences entered Russian culture after the seventeenth century. At a time when icons

were not highly regarded as works of art, Leskov wrote a number
of articles showing a fine appreciation of their esthetic as well as religious qualities. A more immediate stimulus to the writing of the
story came with his acqaintance with a master icon-painter, Nikita
Racheyskov, who preserved the old tradition of painting. Racheyskov was especially noted for his miniatures, "which he executed
with his enormous and seemingly crude hands in a manner as aston-
ishly delicate and subtle as a Chinese."[1] Leskov spent a great deal
of time with Racheyskov absorbing the techniques and the lore of
iconography, and said that he wrote the "Angel" in Racheyskov's
"hot and stuffy studio."

The angel of the title is a small icon depicting a guardian angel,
highly revered by an itinerant band of Old Believer stonemasons.
They carry their angel with them wherever they go and attribute
their good fortune to its influence. The band comes to Kiev to work
on the construction of the first suspension bridge across the Dnepr
River, but they provoke the enmity of a local official who confiscates
their "heretical" icons. Sealing wax is dripped on the angel's face
and the icon marked with an official stamp. The Archbishop of
Kiev, however, is enchanted with this exquisite work of art and
places it on the altar of the cathedral. The Old Believers' attempts
to retrieve their icon create the suspense in the story. Their plan is
to find a suitable icon-painter who could make an identical copy of
the angel and then to steal the original, leaving the copy in its
place. The seeking out of the icon-painter Sevastyan and the pur-
loining of the original, during which Luka, the group's leader, carries the icon across the Dnepr walking on the chains of the still incomplete bridge, are dramatic events skillfully narrated.

The narrative is set in a frame; it is told with sober dignity by one
of the Old Believers, Mark Aleksandrov, in a language wonderfully
combining archaisms, bookish terms, and earthy popular expressions. This gives the story a sense of veracity in spite of some of the
improbabilities of the plot.[2]

Although the story was an immense success and, together with
Cathedral Folk, won Leskov the attention and admiration of a
whole new circle of readers, contemporary critics (notably Dostoevsky[3]) objected to its ending. When the copy of the icon is returned to the church, Luka is shocked to find that the seal which
had been placed on it shortly before to make it perfectly identical
with the original has miraculously vanished. This "miracle" has a
quite prosaic explanation, but Luka interprets it as a sign that he

must abandon his Old Belief. He confesses all to the archbishop, who graciously receives him and the members of his band into the official church. This ending is not as improbable as might appear: given the primitive nature of the Old Believer's faith, an apparent miracle together with the kindness shown by the archbishop could easily move them to abandon their faith. Neither is the ending totally unexpected, since the narrator, Mark, announces at the very beginning that he will tell of how he was led to the true path by an angel. Midway through the story, while seeking the icon-painter Sevastyan, Mark enconters the holy hermit Pamva, and is moved by the spiritual strength and goodness of this representative of the official church. "If there are but two such men in the church," he says, "then we [the Old Believers] are lost, for he is inspired by love." (4. 365). Pamva's example shakes Mark's faith, already weakened by the Old Believers he has met in Moscow, who appear totally mercenary and corrupt. All this, together with the kindness and tolerance of an English couple who aid the Old Believers, is enough to win him over.

But though the ending is logically and psychologically motivated, it is nonetheless esthetically unsatisfying. Had the Old Believers been portrayed as narrow-minded fanatics, their conversion to a religion of greater tolerance and love might have struck a truer note. But they appear as honest, industrious, upright men with a deep love and knowledge of iconography who simply want to be left in peace to continue their religious practices. They seem to have little need for conversion. Leskov later suggested that the ending had been forced on him by Katkov.[4] Considering the doubts about official Orthodoxy expressed in other works Leskov was writing at the time (*Cathedral Folk*, "The Enchanted Pilgrim"), as well as evidence within the story itself, it would appear that Leskov's original intention was to have his Old Believers arrive at a nondogmatic, humane form of Christianity, but not necessarily be slipped so neatly through the doors of the official church. His saintly hermit Pamva, for instance, although nominally Orthodox, has little "official" in his religion: his forest hut contains no icons at all nor any weighty tomes of sacred writings. When he learns of the Old Believers' quest to retrieve their angel, he says: "The angel lives in the hearts of men; he has been sealed by ignorance, but love will smash the seal" (4. 366). Leskov's point, suggested but not fully realized in the story, concerns the real function of icons, in which their religious significance is combined with their esthetic value.

Mark is moved from a purely superstitious awe of the supposed
wonder-working properties of the icon to a deep appreciation of its
beauty, as his description of it in chapter 2 proves. For him it represents a higher ideal, a symbol of faith which gives meaning to life.
Pamva suggests that this ideal in fact is "within the hearts of men."
By the end of the story, Mark himself has come to this realization.
The story thus affirms the highest and most serious purpose for art:
to inspire people with the worthiest of ideals by unsealing the angel
which lives within their hearts.

"Ocharovannyi strannik" (The Enchanted Pilgrim) is another of
Leskov's masterpieces too little appreciated by contemporary
critics. In 1873 Katkov refused to publish it in *Russky vestnik*, regarding it as "raw material" rather than a finished work. Some
years later the critic Nikolay Mikhaylovsky objected to its "lack of
any center whatsoever" and compared its many incidents to a
string of beads, each existing independently from the others. To be
sure, the work contains enough incident to fill several conventional
novels, but there is most definitely a center, and the incidents are
arranged with great skill so that they do develop in a logical pattern. This may not be immediately evident, however, because of the
technique of narration. The story is told by Ivan Flyagin, a man of
immense vitality and spiritual depth but with limited powers of
analysis. As a narrator he is not fully "reliable," in the sense that
he simply relates his life's story as a jumble of highly colorful incidents, attributing things he cannot understand to the action of
divine forces. Flyagin's lack of understanding of his own adventures often creates a fine irony, but a closer analysis of his story reveals that the "beads" which make up the plot are strung in a most
artful and conscious manner.[5] Flyagin often takes literally what his
listeners and readers must see symbolically if they are to make sense
of his life's story. He is convinced, for instance, that the events of
his own life happen not of their own accord but have been largely
predetermined by his mother's vow that her son should enter a
monastery. Until he does so, he believes, he will suffer but not die,
although he will be at the point of death many times. Although this
"enchantment" is a fine device for arousing and sustaining the
reader's curiosity, it is misleading if taken literally. But his life can
be seen symbolically in these terms as a quest for salvation and
the events he relates form definite stages in his progress to this end.[6]

The frame which opens the story neatly introduces its main
themes. A group of tourists sailing across Lake Ladoga find that

the rugged Karelian landscape is so wild and desolate as to drive a man to despair and suicide. Flyagin is introduced and relates the story of an alcoholic Moscow priest whose position is so hopeless that he resolves to kill himself so as to compel his bishop to provide for his destitute family. But the priest is stopped from this when he thinks of the fate of his immortal soul. He then devotes himself, contrary to church law, to prayers for the souls of suicides. The priest's story — of self-sacrifice by *not* committing suicide because of concern for one's salvation — is a major theme of the work as a whole. The second part of the frame completes the introduction of the main themes. Flyagin announces that he is a *koneser*,[7] a man with exceptional talent for breaking wild horses. Flyagin admires the spirit of such animals but realizes that they must be tamed if they are to be of any use. His technique explains his success: "I'd grab his ear as hard as I could with my left hand and with all my strength I'd pull it to one side, and with my right fist I'd give him such a thump between the ears and grind my teeth at him in such a terrifying way that sometimes even his brains would start coming out of his nostrils along with the blood. Well of course after that he would be as gentle as a lamb" (4. 391). But Flyagin in careful not to dominate the beast so totally as to break its spirit. He describes one exceptionally wild stallion which he broke but which died short-ly thereafter because "he couldn't get over his own character" (4. 393). Flyagin's own quest for salvation can be seen in much the same terms: his nature is as wild and ungovernable as the stallions he is so skilled at breaking. His life's adventures are analogous to the process by which he tames horses; his energies must be channeled to a positive purpose but his spirit left unbroken.

Flyagin's story, as V. S. Pritchett has written, is about "primi-tive energy,"[8] the basic life force which contains the potential for both goodness and destruction, the force which compels one to go on living even under the most desperate conditions. The unusual series of incidents which opens the story illustrates this primitive energy at work and reveals the contradictory aspects of Flyagin's character. He whips a monk asleep on a haycart whereupon the horses bolt and the monk is thrown off and killed. Flyagin does not explain his action, but the circumstances — the fine summer day, the lovely countryside — fill him with an exuberance which can find its outlet only in senseless violence. But Flyagin is equally cap-able of thoughtlessly risking his own life to save another's, as he proves when he is almost killed while saving the life of his master and family. His tenderness and unthinking cruelty are illustrated in the episodes describing his concern for his doves, followed by his torture of his mistress's cat. He can be affectionately devoted to the child he is given to nurse while maliciously provoking a duel with a haughty officer. The excruciating scene of his flogging match with the Tatar demonstrates his capacity both to inflict and to suffer pain.

The low point of his biography occurs when he is kept prisoner by the Tatars and literally brought to his knees. The Tatar captivity and the incidents which preceded it have been challenges which forced him to curb his exuberance as he himself has curbed the wildness of the horses he tamed. His sufferings to this point have been for his own transgressions, but after his escape he begins his progress to a new goal — suffering for the sins of others. His encounter with the "magnetizer" who cures him of his fondness for drink is a crucial one. For all its farcicality, this episode conceals a very serious point, as do many other comic scenes in the work. The magnetizer explains in literal terms what Flyagin does metaphorically in later life. The magnetizer continues to drink, he says, because it is his duty to do so: "It's a very difficult calling, my friend, and even quite impossible for many; but I have trained myself for it because I see that one must bear one's lot and I bear mine" (4. 459). He cannot drop the habit, he explains, because someone else might "pick it up": "And as for you, if you suffer from some sort of passion, you mustn't just drop it of your own account in case some other man might pick it up and suffer torments from it. But seek out a man who would take this weakness from you of his own free will" (4. 460). The magnetizer thus takes on Flyagin's drinking habit (an excessive burden, it seems, since he dies of drink shortly thereafter). The magnetizer episode also leads neatly to the next stage of his journey, the awakening of love. Flyagin must first be brought to an awareness of beauty, which to this point he has recognized only in horses. But his encounter with the gypsy girl Grusha reveals a new world to him. His attraction to her is at first only an enchantment with her art and a fascination with her physical beauty, but eventually through her he experiences for the first time love in the form of *agape* rather than *eros*. She can no longer bear to live after the Prince has begun to betray her and must either kill him or herself but can bring herself to do neither. She makes Flyagin swear that he will kill her since he will have the opportunity to repent and save his own soul. Thus, as the magnetizer advised, he takes on her sin and suffers for it. He continues his role when he takes the place of the only son of an elderly couple who is to be sent to the army and risks his life, hoping to expiate the sin of murdering Grusha. His role as scapegoat is played literally when he, dressed in goatskins, performs as the Devil in pre-Lenten carnivals and is beaten by the other actors. After all of these adventures his entry into the monastery (where significantly, he is given the name of Ishmael) comes almost as an anticlimax. His monastic life, although not without its farcical side, does develop his urge for self-sacrifice to its utmost. He learns more about his country and at the end of the story is about to leave the monastery to fulfill his urge to sacrifice his life for his people. As the magnetizer told him earlier, "We, the possessed, suffer so that it should be easier for the rest" (4. 460).

Implicit in all this is an undercurrent of criticism of a church which invests too much in the letter and too little in the spirit of Christianity. The story of the priest who prays for suicides suggests that Christian mercy, if it is to be genuine, must be extended to all. The Orthodox missionaries who refuse to help Flyagin because he is already "saved" by his baptism supply another such example. Flyagin himself, quite unconsciously, provides further evidence that the church's view of mercy is too narrow. He has been brought up in the conventional religion and has primitive faith based on ritual coupled with narrowminded scorn for other faiths. He refuses to recognize the children of his Tatar wives, for instance, since they have not been baptized. Yet on occasions when he allows himself to be guided by love, he violates the acknowledged norms of the church in favor of genuine mercy. The best and most paradoxical example of this is his murder of Grusha, done out of genuine love and pity when he finds the only way he can save her is by killing her.

Ultimately, the "enchantment" of the pilgrim is the enchantment of life itself in which, as the monk in his dream prophesied, he would suffer much adversity, but not die until he had worked out his destiny and in so doing saved himself. The complex but very artful structure of the story beneath its apparent artlessness, the depth of Flyagin's character which exemplifies the Russian character as a whole, the marvelous language of the narrative, make this work one of the high points in Leskov's art.[9]

The search for a positive hero and the attempt to depict a basic, living form of Christianity are again the motives behind "Na kraiu

sveta" (At the World's Edge, 1875). Leskov based this story on incidents from the life of Bishop Nil of Yaroslavl, who worked as a
missionary in Siberia in the 1850s. The plot of the story, concerning
a man who sets out to bring enlightenment to the heathen only to
find that he is in greater need of it than they are, is not exactly
novel, but Leskov's treatment of it produced another masterpiece.
The aged bishop who narrates Leskov's story recalls his first assign-
ment to a distant Siberian diocese and his zealous attempts to raise
the level of the local clergy. Missionary work among the primitive
Yakut nomads of his diocese seemed to be particularly lagging. The
bishop seeks advice from Father Kiriak, a Siberian veteran, but
Father Kiriak's advice is to limit the church's activities to basic education and provide a good example of behavior for the native population. He adamantly refuses to do any missionary work, claiming
that the church's efforts to baptize the natives only harm them. The
bishop decides that he must make a personal visit to the mission
field and sets off on a long trek across the snows with Father Kiriak
and two native guides. But they are caught in a fierce blizzard and
the bishop and his guide are left without provisions. The bishop is
not surprised when his pagan guide abandons him, and he resigns
himself to death. But to his amazement, this same pagan risks his
life to return with food and save his companion.

   What Leskov does here once again is to contrast the cold religion
of the church, intent on saving souls by reliance on the sacraments,
with the living spirit of religion exemplified by the unnamed
"heathen" guide. Leskov does this in a subtle and convincing manner, and produces a penetrating critique of established Christianity.
The opening frame of the story already introduces his theme unobtrusively. The bishop narrator shows a group of visitors his collection of artistic portrayals of Christ, discussing each one in turn. He
tells his listeners that the only artist who captured the true spirit of
Christianity is the anonymous master who painted the icon which
stands in his room. Although this image lacks the sophistication
and refinement of later Western portrayals, in its unassuming simplicity and total sincerity it conveys the real essence of Christ's
teachings. The story contains a certain mockery of the established
church's efforts to make this essentially simple doctrine into something mysterious and complex. Father Kiriak, for example, explains to the bishop the impossibility of trying to convey to the natives such concepts as "martyr" and "baptist." "It is still more difficult to talk about the merits of the sacred blood of Christ," he

says, "or about other mysteries of the faith, and it is quite pointless to construct some sort of theological system for them or even to mention the idea of virgin birth without a husband. Either they will understand nothing, which is the best that could happen, or else they will simply laugh in your face" (5. 468). The bishop persists in trying to explain the fundamentals of Orthodoxy to his guide and despairs at the latter's total lack of comprehension. He feels only scorn and pity for this poor "savage" who is, it seems, to be denied salvation. Better, thinks the bishop, that these hopeless people become extinct like the Aztecs. The guide refuses to be baptized: for not only will this earn him the enmity of rival religious groups, the Buddhists and the Shamans, but, he explains, those who are baptized can no longer be trusted. Baptism is like a license to commit crime since the baptized know that the priest will absolve them of any sins. The guide argues that the priest can only forgive those who have done some injury to him personally. The guide's only conception of Christianity is that Christ was a good and a merciful man. It is only after the story's reversal that the bishop understands that his "savage" has a far better grasp of the essence of Christianity than does the bishop himself.

Leskov does not idealize his primitive; indeed he emerges as a very human and convincing figure. One of the best scenes in the story is the description of how the two wait out the blizzard huddled together under the snow, breathing on one another for warmth. The bishop is grateful for warmth, but would gladly sacrifice it because of the stench from his guide, compounded of "stinking reindeer hide, pungent human sweat, smoke, damp putrefaction, dried fish, fish oil, and dirt..." while his resounding snores "like the buzzing of a dense and powerful swarm of bees in a resonant, dry hive, softly beating against its walls" prevent him from sleeping (5. 491–93). These vivid touches help remove any aura of sentimentality which might surround this noble savage. Yet a series of symbols, subtly interwoven into a fabric of the story, makes it plain that the pagan guide embodies that very ideal of brotherly love toward which Christianity strives. The smybolism underlines his role, ironically enough, as the one who enlightens the would-be missionary. Among the few things the guide knows about Christ is that he once gave sight to a blind man by rubbing spittle on his eyes and that he miraculously fed the people with bread and fishes. After their first night in the blizzard, the bishop awakens in panic, unable to see because his eyelids have frozen shut. The guide restores his sight by spitting on his eyes and rubbing them. The cavity in the snow where the two wait out the blizzard seems like a grave to the bishop, and the stench from his guide worse than that of Lazarus after his four days in the tomb at Bethany. He has resigned himself to death and indeed, when his guide returns after four days, he scarcely knows whether he is alive or dead. The reappearance of the guide and the bishop's return to life seem to him truly miraculous; his hunger, fatigue, and the uncertain light of the short Siberian day play tricks with his vision. He sees a figure approaching which seems to "materialize" in the form of an angel. It is the guide, covered with frost, his hair piled high on his head and coated with ice (he left his hat as a pledge in the deserted *yurt* where he took food). "Toward me floated a gigantic winged figure enveloped from head to foot in a *chiton* of sparkling silver brocade; he wore an enormous headdress which appeared to be almost six feet high, a headdress which burned as if it were all encrusted with jewels, or as if it were a solid miter of jewels..." (5. 505-6). There seems little doubt that the "savage" — by restoring the bishop's sight, by wondrously providing him with food, and by giving him back his life — has worked miracles as genuine as any described in the Gospels.

The reversal in the story is all the more effective since the bishop is portrayed as a sensible and enlightened if perhaps overzealous man, but not as a bigoted fanatic. He now understands that "Christ has revealed Himself to him [the guide] as much as is necessary..." (5. 510) and abandons his proselytizing. Amid the empty Siberian landscape, "at the world's edge," where nature is stripped to its very minimum, the bishop finds the essence of religion, a faith also stripped to its very minimum. This was the simplified form of Christianity which Leskov had arrived at after his trip abroad in 1875, a faith founded on brotherly love, with a system of ethics much broader than that of institutionalized Christianity (exemplified here by one who is formally a pagan). The beliefs expressed in the story anticipate those of Tolstoy.

II *Unorthodox Views of Orthodoxy*

Several other stories of the 1870s, although not of the caliber of the three discussed above, also explore highly unconventional attitudes to religion. "Vladychnyi sud" (Episcopal Justice, 1877) was written immediately after "At the World's Edge" and is linked directly to it. But its overall tone is startlingly different and appears to go counter to the humane and tolerant view of the earlier story. Leskov begins by explaining that, in spite of its popularity among readers, "At the World's Edge" was criticized by the clergy for its "tolerance of unbelief and even indifference toward Holy Baptism as a means of salvation" (6. 88).

To prove that his bishop's very liberal views were by no means unique among the clergy, he relates a story in the form of an incident from his own youth, when he had served in the Recruiting Section in Kiev in the 1850s. At that time the law allowed recruitment of Jewish boys into the army as early as the age of twelve. If, as was usually the case, no records of birth could be produced, the evidence of witnesses was sufficient to establish the boy's age. Such witnesses often made a profession of giving false testimony, thereby sending boys of seven or eight for military service. A Jewish bookbinder appears to Leskov one day in an agony of worry because his young son is about to be taken as a recruit. The father has, quite legally, paid for a replacement for his son, but only after selling all his possessions to do so. The replacement is about to cheat the father out of his due by requesting baptism into the Orthodox faith. This would free him from his obligation since the law allowed only a Jew to take the place on another Jew. Ultimately, it is Metropolitan Filaret of Kiev who solves the dilemma by deciding that the replacement is unworthy of baptism, thus ensuring that the boy will be spared.

Leskov provides a glowing tribute to Filaret, hailing his "infinite goodness" and supplying a number of anecdotes to show his human side. Yet the anecdotes do little more than make him appear a good-natured fool. Filaret's decision likewise seems scarcely more than elementary human decency. But what is even more peculiar, even distasteful, is Leskov's own role in the story, specifically his attitude toward the grief-stricken father. Leskov admits he was deeply moved by the man's plight and conveys the father's utter desperation (he literally sweats blood). But he spares no opportunity to ridicule the Jew by painting him as some sort of subhuman creature, using the stereotyped devices of the crudest anti-Semitic propaganda of the day. In a farcical and unnecessary scene, he portrays the Jew fleeing in terror from a bulldog that he believes is a crocodile. When the Jew follows him home to implore him to help, Leskov allows him to spend the night curled up on the floor next to the dog. "I was satisfied with both the Jew and the dog," he remarks, "and left them to share their common pallet until morning..." (6. 116).

A solution occurred to him when he first learned of the Jew's plight — both father and son should themselves be baptized. But he does not suggest this to anyone, and indeed forgets the whole affair until by chance he is reminded of it on the following day and tells an acquaintance who intercedes with Metropolitan Filaret. Leskov's attempts to justify this lack of concern are revealing: he stresses that he was raised in a devout Orthodox family and from an early age was inculcated with the conventional attitudes of such a milieu. His reluctance to save the Jew through baptism stemmed from his respect for the sacrament and his unwillingness to see it improperly used. It would thus appear that he wishes to jolt his readers into greater awareness by showing in himself the unthinking anti-Semitism of the typical Russian of his day, whose concern for maintaining respect for the purely formal rites of the church overrides his feelings of elementary humanity. The passages describing the Jew as a very human, suffering father are presumably intended to shatter the blindly prejudiced, stereotyped view. But the technique simply does not work. Leskov's own motivations are never made clear, and his mockery of the Jew — even with the best intentions — remains distasteful.[10]

The story has other flaws as well. There is a good deal of irrelevant memoir material describing various people and events in Kiev in the 1850s which in intended to increase the tension by retarding the climax. But in such a story it serves only to distract from the very powerful central episode. An epilogue in which Leskov meets this same Jew some years later to find that he has now become a zealous convert to Orthodoxy is an unnecessary touch which also mars the story.

In "Nekreshchenyi pop" (The Unbaptized Priest, 1877) Leskov again uses baptism as a means to distinguish the spirit of religion from its purely formalistic side. In contrast to the preceding stories, he writes here in a comic mode. The story is set in a Ukrainian village, and portions of it are clearly modeled on Gogol's early stories, with their witches, devils, extramarital escapades, and extensive use of the Ukrainian language. But the good-humored tone and absorbing plot mask some very pointed criticism of the official church. Dukach, an independent and quarrelsome villager, is, after years of childlessness, at last blessed with a son. But his troublesome nature has earned him the enmity of his neighbors, and not one of them will consent to act as godparent for his son. He decides to hold the christening in a neighboring village and sends his none-too-clever nephew Agap along with the village pariah, Kerasivna, who is rumored to be a witch. The two are caught in a severe blizzard during which Dukach accidentally kills Agap. Dukach goes to prison and Kerasivna insists that the child has been properly christened Savva as his father wished. Savva is educated by a kindly man who has been strongly influenced by the Stundists[11] and eventually becomes the priest of his native parish. His good sense and charity win him the love of his parishoners. But on her deathbed Kerasivna confesses that the blizzard forced her to turn back before the christening could take place. The beloved Father Savva, she insists, is not even a Christian, much less a priest. This naturally causes great consternation among the villagers, who wonder if all their marriages, christenings, and confessions are invalid. But they are so devoted to their priest that they insist he remain, and their kindly and sensible bishop agrees.

A very deliberate contrast is drawn between Fr. Savva's activities and those of the quite legally baptized priest in the next parish. While his neighbor concerns himself with building a splendid stone church and acquiring a bell and wonder-working icon for it, Fr. Savva ensures that the orphans of his parish are fed and clothed and that a school is provided for the village. Savva's modest wooden church is full, even though the population of the surrounding area has largely gone over to the Stundists, while the neighboring priest ministers to the verger and the churchmouse. The formal rite of baptism again provides a point from which to launch an attack on a church whose stress on Byzantine ritual sometimes threatened to obscure the essence of Christianity.

The stories of the 1870s discussed above, then, are primarily concerned with demonstrating a system of Christian ethics which, in its simplicity and universality, already anticipates the ideas of Tolstoy, but which is not fully elaborated. The basis of this system is active love for one's fellow man; its ultimate manifestation is self-sacrifice. This system comes increasingly into conflict with the teachings of the established church. Leskov focuses on the sacraments of the church, through them pointing out the narrowness and dogmatism of official Christianity. Artistically, the best of these stories are related as *skaz*, relying on the individualized language of the distinctive narrator to give them life.

III   *The Russian Character*

Many of Leskov's writings deal, in one way or another, with the Russian character,[12] but a group of stories from the late 1870s and early 1880s is specifically devoted to a skeptical examination of the strengths and weaknesses of his countrymen. One technique which Leskov uses to illuminate the Russian character is to focus on an encounter between a foreigner and the Russians. The foreigner does not necessarily provide any standard of behavior by which the Russians are measured; more often it is only his fresh point of view and different standards which make the idiosyncracies of the Russians stand out all the more clearly. Even in his very first newspaper articles at the beginning of the 1860s, Leskov drew comparisons between Russian and foreign practices. The adventures of his uncle Scott (much fictionalized, to be sure) enabled him to make many comments on Russian manners. The Germans are also contrasted with the Russians: the Biedermeyer cosiness of the Norks in *The Islanders* implicitly affirms the value of the family at a time when the institution was under attack from the radicals. Leskov's attitude toward Germans is generally favorable in this novel, and there is no doubt of his admiration for their energy and practicality (although the pompous Friedrich Schultz illustrates some of their less admirable qualities.)

In the 1870s Leskov was disturbed by the rise of German militarism (see the ending of "The Enchanted Pilgrim"), and some personal encounters with Germans in the Baltic left him with a strong distaste for their smugness and chauvinistic scorn for the Russians. The aftermath of the Franco-Prussian War and the rumblings of the Iron Chancellor make up part of the background to a fine satire, "Zheleznaia volia" (A Will of Iron, 1876).

The frame of the story portrays a group of Russians who express their fears that disorganized and undisciplined Russia would not fare well in a conflict with iron-willed Germany. Vochnev, an old man who has followed the discussion without comment, finally disagrees: "Iron they well may be, but we are dough, simple, soft, damp, unbaked dough — and you should remember that dough in a mass cannot be chopped up even with an ax. Indeed, you may well lose the ax" (6. 6). Vochnev then tells a story — loosely based on some of Leskov's own experiences when he worked for Scott and Wilkins — of an encounter between German iron and Russian dough. A German engineer, Hugo Pectoralis, arrives in a small

Russian provincial town to supervise the installation of some agricultural machinery ordered from his firm in Germany. Pectoralis seems almost an accessory to the machinery he has come to install: precise, unyielding, utterly consistent. The quality he most admires in himself is his vaunted "will of iron": once he has set himself a goal he will never go back on his word no matter what the consequences. But his iron will proves to be his nemesis in Russia: after a long series of misadventures, in the course of which he is abandoned by his wife and his promising business is reduced to bankruptcy, he nonetheless keeps his promise to eat pancakes at the funeral of his archenemy, only to be outblinied by a gluttonous priest. The story is well constructed so that Pectoralis's reversals grow ever more serious untill his final tragicomic demise.

Pectoralis is a caricature, of course, but a very successful one. One might expect that with such a ridiculous German at the center of the stage, the Russians in the story would appear as models of virtue. Indeed, a lesser author handling such a situation might easily have sunk into chauvinistic glorification of the Russian character. But the satire is double-edged, with both edges sufficiently honed so that the Russians are spared little more than Pectoralis. As Vochnev suggests at the beginning of the story, the chief advantage of the Russians in any conflict with the Germans is their stupidity, which would utterly confound the Teutonic mania for precision and thorough calculation: "I am not praising my countrymen," he slyly remarks, "nor am I censuring them: I am only saying that they will hold their own and, whether through intelligence or stupidity, they will manage to defend themselves" (6. 7). The Russian character emerges as a total, and scarcely favorable, contrast to the German, exemplified by Pectoralis: where he is industrious, they are lazy; he is firm, they are yielding; he is restrained and frugal while they spend lavishly; he is calculating, they are instinctively cunning. Yet Pectoralis's virtures are so exaggerated that he functions with coldly mechanical precision and predictability, whereas the Russians' vices at least make them warmly human.

Leskov was a master at relating with malicious glee the downfall of an innocent, often a foreigner, as he is inexorably swallowed up by Russian life. But he does portray the Russians here "without praise and without censure"; apart from Chekhov, no nineteenth-century writer regarded his countrymen with fewer illusions than Leskov.

"Besstydnik" (A Man Without Shame, 1877) employs the same

framing device as the previous story: in this case, a group of naval
officers discusses life at sea as a means of developing character.
One tells a story to illustrate the influence of environment on character which contains as dubious a compliment to the Russians as
does "A Will of Iron." His story is set immediately after the Crimean War, when revelations of widespread corruption in the
army's supply services outraged front-line veterans in particular.
Once at an evening of cards the narrator began to abuse supply officers as parasites and thieves who filled their pockets while honest
soldiers suffered and died at the front. His rage does not subside
when he discovers that a supply officer is sitting near him. The supply officer not only listens to the tirade with equanimity, but even
takes some pride in providing further examples of how well he and
his fellow officers profited from the war. Although unmoved by
the attacts on his profession, he does take the narrator to task for
insulting the Russian people as a whole: "We are all Russians," he
insists, "and we all have been given as part of our rich nature the
capacity to cope with any circumstances. . . . You were given the
task of fighting and this you did the best way possible — you
fought and died as heroes and your fame has spread all over
Europe. But we are placed in a position where we could steal, and
we, too, distinguished ourselves and stole enough to become renowned. But if, for example, we were ordered to change places and
we went to the trenches and you to supply-points, then, we thieves
would have fought and died and you would have. . .   stolen"
(6. 157–58). After twenty years of life experience, the narrator is
forced to admit that the supply officer was right.

"Chertogon" (Exorcising the Devil, 1879) is a brief story superb-
ly illustrating some contradictory traits of the Russian character. It
describes a "rite which can be seen only in Moscow" (6. 302): a
wealthy merchant, driven by his demon of boredom and dissatis-
faction with life, stages a tremendous orgy during which a restaurant dining room is utterly ravaged. The next day, after a bath and
haircut, he prostrates himself on the floor of a church and prays
with such intensity that his legs shudder spasmodically. At last he
rises and announces that he has been forgiven: "Right from the
very top of the church," he says, "I felt an open hand reach down
from the cupola, grasp me by the hair, and set me right on my feet
again" (6. 314). Although the merchant pays the 17,000 ruble bill
in the restaurant with little hesitation, he delays his morning break
for tea until joined by colleagues because the tavern gives groups of

three a five kopek discount. Leskov manages, through careful selection of telling detail, to convey both the fury of the orgy and the fervor of the merchant's prayers. The point of view (the story is told by the merchant's naive young nephew, fresh from the provinces) adds to the effect. "Since then," the narrator concludes slyly, "I have come to know the national manner of falling so that one can rise again" (6. 314).

"Levsha" (Lefty [The Tale of the Cross-Eyed Left Handed Craftsman of Tula and the Steel Flea]) is another ambiguous tribute to the Russian character. Its original edition of 1881 was accompanied by a preface in which Leskov stated that he had recorded this "legend from the armory" from the works of an old craftsman of the Sestroretsk arms factory. The story had such an air of authenticity that one critic accused Leskov of simply acting as a stenographer. Only later did he reveal that, apart from the basic idea — summed up in a catch phrase "The English made a Steel flea but our Tula lads shod it and sent it back again" — the whole story was his own invention. More recent Soviet scholarship has confirmed this, but has also uncovered several possible historical prototypes of the craftsman and sources of some of the episodes.[13]

"Lefty" is one of Leskov's best known stories and, unfortunately, the one most likely to be fatally injured in translation.[14] The plot itself — the adventures of the Tula gunsmith who manages to outdo the English and preserve Russia's pride by putting shoes on the life-sized steel flea which the English have created to demonstrate the high standard of their craftsmanship — is outrageous enough, but the language in which all this is related is even more extravagant. Purely invented words (the marvelous *nimfozoria*), complex puns, mangled foreign words misused or wittily combined with Russian ones (*melkoskop* for "microscope," from *melkii*, "fine," "small"; *kleveton* for "feuilleton," from *kleveta*, "slander") make the story all but untranslatable. Leskov explained the motivation of such language elsewhere: "The language is dotted with capricious agglomerations of improperly used words from the most varied contexts. This arises, or course, from the overly assiduous attempts of the storytellers to hit upon the conversational tone of that social stratum from whence they take their characters. Deprived of the possibility of acquiring the real form of conversational language of these people, they attempt to achieve it through maximum vivacity in their retelling, putting as colorful and as fanciful speech as possible into the mouths of their characters so that it should be unlike the language of everyday'' (7. 60–61). This explanation of course only partially accounts for Leskov's decision to use the language he did. He had an immense love of words in themselves, and the story can be seen as an attempt to uncover more of their full potential. But the language does give the story a sparkle and verve impossible to convey fully in translation. Leskov succeeds in doing with words what his legendary craftsman did in metal: he creates a unique and highly amusing curiosity, but one which also has a bite that the famous steel flea did not have.

There is no doubt of Leskov's admiration for the unacknowledged and often untutored craftsmen who delighted in pushing their skills to the limits of the seemingly impossible. He was enchanted, for example, with the skill of the Palekh icon-painters ''who can portray distinctly, on an icon measuring three and one-half by four and one-half inches, 129 figures along with ornamentation, walls, mountains, the Garden of Paradise, graves and Hell, where angels beat and enchain 'Satan and all his angels.' And around the head of each of these 129 figures is an aureole of gold, within which is a title: 'St. Iliya,' 'St. Enokh,' 'St. Rakh, the Robber,' etc. These inscriptions are so minute that they are difficult to read and not everyone can do so with the naked eye.''[15] The idea of the steel flea itself may be nothing more than a tall story, but the skill which shod it was real enough and Leskov pays it due tribute. The craftsman himself is not without his positive significance (indeed, Leskov included the story in his cycle of righteous men), and his gentle mockery of Lefty's naiveté and backwardness still leaves no doubt that the craftsman is quite sincerely concerned about the welfare of his country.

The saga of the steel flea in intended to deflate the Russians' pride in their capacity to surpass the West purely on the basis of instinct or innate ability, without painstaking and systematic work. The marvelous achievement of the Tula craftsmen obscures the fact that in shoeing the steel flea they have ruined its delicate mechanism, since the shoes are too heavy. As one of the Englishmen remarks when the Russians triumphantly return the newly shod curiosity: ''You would be better off knowing at least the four ways of reckoning by 'rithmetic. . . Then you could figure out that each machine can only do things 'cording to its power. You are mightly clever with your hands, but you didn't count on the fact that such a little gadget as this *nimfozoria* here has been worked out even to the most exact precisity and it can't carry no horseshoes. On account of that this *nimforzoria* won't skip around any more and don't even dance the *dansé*" (7. 49–50). Leskov would not dispute with those who saw his Lefty as a symbol of the Russian people as a whole, adding that he had no wish either to flatter or to ridicule his countrymen. The thrust of his satire is against the backwardness of his country and the belief in the special talents inherent in the Russian character which was often used to excuse that backwardness.

Despite his talent and his love for his country, Lefty is a victim of his own nationality. His fondness for drink begins his downfall, and the system he collides with in his own country completes it. His treatment on return from England pointedly contrasts with that accorded to an Englishman with whom he had a drinking bout on the way back to Russia. The Englishman is taken to his embassy, where he is treated by a doctor and an apothecary, is given pills of guttapercha and a drink of *heure-fixe*, and left to sleep it off in a comfortable bed. Lefty, on the other hand is dumped on the floor of the police station, grilled about his passport, and, after the police have relieved him of his money and his "tripeter" watch, is sent off to die in a paupers' hospital.

There is yet one more barb to Leskov's satire: simply because the English have done something absurd (making a mechanized steel flea), the Russians feel obliged to outdo them with something even more absurd (putting shoes on it). Thus Leskov manages simultaneously to ridicule what might be termed the "Slavophile" view of Russia's destiny, with its obscurantist belief in the special talents of the Russians, as well as the "Westernizer" approach, with its uncritical assumption that everything coming from the West is good and should be adopted and improved upon in Russia. Even the language of the story, with its lexicon of undigested terms from several European languages, conveys this. The narrator's attempts to achieve a high tone in his speech are as laughable as are the frantic efforts of his countrymen to outdo the West.

Leskov at one time planned a series of tales similar to "Lefty," but the series, entitled "Historical Character in Fabulous Tales of Recent Composition," has only one other member, "Leon, dvoretskii syn" (Leon, the Steward's Son, 1881). Although it contains much clever word play, the story as a whole has less verve than "Lefty" and the display of verbal fireworks too often becomes simply an end in itself.

"Kolyvan'skii muzh" (A Kolyvan Husband, 1888) is another story in which a naive, weak-willed, but likable character is slowly drawn into a net of circumstances which renders him helpless. As in "A Will of Iron," Leskov deals with the meeting of German iron and Russian dough, but this time the dough is thoroughly kneaded, formed, and baked into a neat *Brötchen*. Sipachev, a young naval officer, begins as the most Russian of Russians: he is born in Kaluga of an old family, and his father and uncle are ardent Slavophiles. In Reval (whose old Russian name was Kolyvan') he marries into a charming and cultured German family. His relatives are aghast, fearing he will lose his national identity, but they become reconciled to the marriage when he assures them that he will have a son, Nikita, to be raised as a good Orthodox and carry on the family name. But his German kin arrange for him to be away on duty whenever a child is due, and each time he returns he finds he has fathered a Gottfried, then an Oswald, and finally a Gunther, each baptized as a Lutheran. Sipachev himself ends as a good German and is buried in a Lutheran cemetary in Dresden.

Although the story has many pages which sparkle with wry humor, it lacks the fine irony of "A Will of Iron." Leskov's satirical impulses overflow to such an extent that the point of the story is not altogether clear. He no doubt had in mind the practice of baptizing Russian children in the Baltic area as Germans, a topic which had been noted in the press. There is little anti-German satire of any force: the Germans in the story are cultivated and not openly chauvinistic, but they are also so convinced of their own superiority that they cannot understand why anyone would not want to become a German. The Russian will to retain national identity is weak as well. "We are monkeys," warns Sipachev's uncle, "and we love to imitate" (8. 409). But Leskov also assaults Russian chauvinism, especially that of the Slavophiles with their insistence on forced Russification of the Baltic provinces. He mocks their ideas and even their speech, which he reproduces as an archaic Russian heavily laden with Old Church Slavonicisms. Sipachev's own flabby will is another target. Thus the story's overall impact is reduced through diffusion.

This group of stories reveals Leskov's thorough knowledge of the Russian character and his healthily skeptical view of his countrymen. His tone of detached, wry amusement and his technique of simultaneously poking fun at the quirks of both the Russians and the foreigners give his works objectivity and universality. The choice of topic is also significant: the mood of society was growing increasingly chauvinistic in the later 1870s, and Leskov's attempts to deflate the excess pride of his countrymen once again set him against the current of his times.

CHAPTER 5

Stories and Tales II: The Positive Ideal

I *The Righteous Men*

I N the late 1870s Leskov began a series of stories grouped under
the general title of "Pravedniki" (Righteous Men). His own explanation of his motivation is interesting, even if not fully revealing. He describes an amusing encounter with his friend, the writer Alexei Pisemsky, who justified the numerous scoundrels and villians in his (Pisemsky's) writings on the grounds that he simply described what he saw. This set Leskov to thinking: "Is it really possible that all the fine and good things which other writers have portrayed in their works are only fabrications and nonsense?... If no city can stand without three righteous men, as the popular belief has it,[1] then how will our whole land prevail with only the refuse that exists in my soul, and in yours, dear reader?" (6. 642). And so, Leskov continues, he set off to seek out some righteous men. In his earlier writings, of course, he had created many positive characters and eccentrics whose ethical values often ran counter to the prevailing ones. But as Leskov grew increasingly estranged from the official church in the later 1870s, the urge to portray individuals who had evolved their own independent ethical codes grew more pressing. Thus he assembles a series of figures of exceptional moral rectitude from the most diverse areas of life. More often than not, they do not philosophize or preach to others; indeed, they are unconcious of their own worth. His righteous men are heroic, but their heroism arises from the manner in which they live their everyday lives.

As he explained: "To live a long life justly, day in and day out without lying, without deceiving, without conniving, without offending one's neighbor and without censuring one's enemy unfairly — this is much more difficult than to throw oneself into an abyss as did Curtius or to pierce one's breast with a bundle of arrows as did the famous hero of Switzerland's struggle for freedom... 'Chance creates a hero; ... everyday valor a *righteous man.*'... We give our heroes their due esteem, but we place our righteous men immeasurably higher, for we believe that 'only with the increase of the righteous shall the people rejoice.' "[2]

The righteous men are fictional characters, but are modeled on historical or living figures. Some are the humblest sort, others of elevated rank, but all work in fields where it would be difficult to lead a just life. All are colorful, indeed some have become, as Leskov says, "legends." What links them is their sense of duty to their fellow man and, above all, their ability to act on what their conscience tells them.

Leskov's first righteous man, portrayed in "Odnodum" (Singlethought, 1879), is a police officer in a small provincial town in the early part of the century. Ryzhov, the hero, has no qualifications for the post other than his exceptional physical strength. He soon proves, however that it is his moral rather than his physical force which enables him to keep good order in the town. To the utter astonishment of everyone, he not only refuses to take bribes, as is the accepted practice for such functionaries, but will not even accept gifts from the townspeople. He lives on his salary of two rubles, eighty-seven kopeks per month, fulfilling his duties in exemplary fashion. The town governor, dismayed to find that Ryzhov's practices are cutting down on his own income, enlists the aid of the local priest to get rid of the uncorruptible policeman. In a highly ironic passage, the priest tells the governor that Ryzhov's "harmful fantasy" comes from his constant reading of the Bible: "All of the Orthodox of Holy Russia know that one who has read the Bible 'right up to Christ' cannot be truly expected to act reasonably; such people are, however, akin to 'God's fools' — they act the fool but do not harm and are not to be feared" (6.222). Ryzhov himself eventually becomes town governor. When the new provincial governor, Lansky, makes his first inspection (the description of the frenzied preparations for the visit is one of the best parts of the story), Ryzhov's total honesty earns him, not a period of exile in Siberia, but Lansky's respect and the order of St. Vladimir.

Ryzhov, however, remains a cold, stern and distant figure. There is a possibility of revealing something of his inner life, for, like Tuberozov in *Cathedral Folk*, Ryzhov keeps a journal of his thoughts and "prophecies" which he entitles "Singlethought." But we have only a few fragments of this work, and thus know little of Ryzhov himself. This, indeed, is a recurring problem with many of Leskov's righteous men. Leskov is so concerned with the outward image of his heroes, with the practical application of their moral principles, that he pays little attention to their inner drama. They are intended to be larger than life and if Leskov also tried to convey the full scale of their humanity, the image would surely crack under the strain.

The next righteous man, "Nesmertel'nyi Golovan" (Deathless Golovan, 1880), is also portrayed from a distance but moves across a background (Orel of the 1830s) which is teeming with life and color. Here Leskov gathers his material from the oral tradition of the townspeople, from stories told by his own family, and from his childhood memories of a legendary character in the town. Indeed, he says his very first memory is of being saved from certain death from a vicious dog by Golovan himself. Golovan ("Bighead") is a serf who has purchased his own freedom and that of his family. He had served for a time in the Caucasus as the orderly of General Ermolov, who provided him, on leaving the service, with two cows and a copy of Pope's *Essay on Man*. The cows formed the basis of Golovan's living thereafter — providing high quality dairy products for the townspeople — while he had committed Pope to memory and often quotes him fondly. Golovan's total honesty and self-lessness quickly win him the trust and respect of the townspeople who give over to his keeping the deeds to land holdings in his neighborhood and rely on his impartiality for settling disputes. When others seek his advice he tells them to "act as if you might die tomorrow."

Golovan's almost magical aura which causes the townspeople to consider him "deathless" had its origins during an epidemic in Orel when he was the only one who followed his own advice and went about bringing food to the sick as if he had no fear of dying. The legend which surrounds him includes the important detail that when he noticed a plague pustule in his own calf, he promptly cut off the infected flesh and threw it into the river. The townspeople are quick to accept this as a literal sacrifice of himself done to spare the town further ravages of the plague. The only small stain on his character is Pavla, a young woman whom Golovan has taken in after her husband abandoned her. The townspeople refer to her as "Golovan's sin." Only much later does Leskov learn that their love was "perfect" and platonic: Golovan remained a virgin. His conscience would not permit him to marry Pavla since her former husband was alive; in fact he extorted money from Golovan which the latter paid out of love for Pavla.

The superstition which leads the townspeople to make a legend of "Deathless Golovan" is mocked in what appears a lengthy but colorful digression which in fact is essential to the story's meaning. Leskov describes the hordes gathering in expectation of a miracle when some holy relics are displayed in a neighboring town. The only "miracle" which occurs is a complete fraud, perpetrated by Pavla's husband. Leskov's point is that Golovan's whole life, though it exhibited none of the miracles attributed to saints, in fact is far more worthy of reverence than the yellowing bones of a martyr. "Amazing people," he concludes. "Amazing and even improbable. They are improbable while they are surrounded by the fabrications of legend, and they appear even more improbable when one manages to remove the patina from them and to see them in all their saintly simplicity" (6.397).

Several of the stories in the cycle take place during the reign of Nicholas I, a period whose bureaucratic tyranny and barrack-room discipline provided ample setting for conflicts between conscience and duty. In "Pigmei" (The Pigmy, 1876), Leskov presents a minor police clerk who manages, at great personal risk, to save a man wrongly convicted of rape. A suspenseful and well-told story designed to show "what even the least important of men can do for his neighbor when he sincerely wants to help him" (PSS, 3.108), it is unfortunately marred by a sentimental ending. Excess sentimentality also detracts from "Kadetskii monastyr," (The Cadet Monastery, 1880), a series of portraits of staff members of the First Cadet Corps in St. Petersburg. The four heroes, who devote themselves totally to the moral and physical welfare of the cadets, are so idealized that they are scarcely credible. "Inzhenery-bessrebrenniki" (Unmercenary Engineers, 1887) also deals with an officer, Fermor, who attempts to live by the highest of Christian ideals while on active service in the army. Fermor, however, only manages to convince his brother officers that he is mad and ends in suicide. In recreating the lives of these obscure historical figures, Leskov hoped to balance his contemporaries' view of the past by showing them some good men, who, "standing outside the mainstream of history. . . make history more than do any others" (6.347). Although he manages to capture the flavor of Nicholas I's iron rule, his heroes are flat and colorless and fail to convince.

"Sheramur" (Cheramour, 1879) is a story as curious as its title. Leskov did not originally include it in the cycle, but eventually published it in a separate edition, *Three Righteous Men and One Cheramour* (1880), and included it with his "Righteous Men" in his *Collected Works*. It is very different in tone and in subject matter (the only work of the cycle with a contemporary setting), yet it does belong here. "Cheramour" is the story of a curious Russian emigré whom Leskov encountered in Paris in 1875. His nickname is a gallicized corruption of Chernomor, the malicious dwarf of Pushkin's narrative poem *Ruslan and Lyudmila*, a name given to him because of his long and bushy black beard and his small stature. His growth was stunted, he says, because as a child he never had enough to eat, so that food is now his obsession. He is a "hero of the belly," concerned not only with his own digestion but with ensuring that others are fed as well. After a series of ludicrous, mildly salacious, and occaionally heroic episodes, he finds his niche in life as the husband of Tante Grillade, proprietress of a cheap eating house in the Latin Quarter who sees that he is well fed and allows him to stage banquets for the beggars of Paris.

Cheramour's ideal seems scarcely to harmonize with the saintly self-denial of the other righteous men, and yet his concern with only the very basics of life, his total ignorance of politics and religion, and his utter candor provide a welcome relief from the cold holiness of Leskov's other heroes. No doubt this is one reason why the story was included in the cycle. Yet Cheramour can make his own claim to righteousness. One episode of the story depicts a Radstockite Countess who undertakes to "save" him and only begins to feed him when she is convinced that he has found salvation. Her unfeeling, superficial piety makes Cheramour's own unconscious goodness and instinctive generosity and utter lack of concern for his own welfare all the more evident. The fact that Cheramour can live a truly righteous life with apparently no higher ideal than "to eat" (*zhrat'*) is intended to cast doubt upon the more recondite preoccupations of organized religion and to strengthen Leskov's case for a simplified and basic form of Christianity. Cheramour is indeed the wise fool (*chreva-radi iurodivyi*) whose behavior exposes the folly of the sane. The technique of the story — much of it is told from Cheramour's naive point of view using his mangled vocabulary and unintentional puns — also gives it an air of veracity and warmth.

"Pugalo" (The Bogey-Man, 1885) stands somewhat apart from the other stories of the cycle. It was originally published as a Christmas story for children, and exhibits some of the typical features of this genre. There is, for example, an air of mystery and lurking evil intended to raise at least a few hairs on little heads listening as the story was read by the fireside. The fears are not raised simply as effects but are central to the story's meaning. It is cast as Leskov's personal recollection of events from his childhood and concerns an outcast, Selivan, rumored to be an archcriminal and sorcerer. In fact Selivan is a sterling character who rescues the narrator from an accident and who has devoted himself to the care of another outcast, a hangman's daughter whom the townspeople also ostracized.

Such a well-worn plot acquires new life in Leskov's telling, and even the clearly stated moral at the end seems quite appropriate. The point of view in the story is also effectively shifted from that of the child, whose head is filled with the superstitions of the adults he encounters, to the adult narrator gently mocking his own childhood fears of the dreaded Selivan. As in many of the other stories of the cycle, we see little of the central figure, Selivan, himself; the stress is rather on the popular opinion of him. But the technique works well here since it is public opinion itself which is of concern. Prejudice is defeated and virtue triumphs, and in a convincing manner.

"Figura" (1889) is likewise told as a personal memoir, this time from Leskov's Kiev days, when he encountered an ex-army officer who lived like a peasant, raising fruits and vegetables on his small plot. Figura (a corruption of the hero's surname, Vigura) relates an episode from his army days reminiscent of one told by Father Zosima in *The Brothers Karamazov*. He was once struck by one of his men, a Cossack so drunk he did not know what he was doing. Figura does not respond by killing the Cossack, as military custom dictated, but listens to his conscience which tells him to forgive the man. His superiors regard this as a stain upon his honor and he is compelled to retire from the service. This is a slim basis for a story and Leskov attempts to flesh it out by portraying Figura's idyllic form of life (a pastoral ideal which runs through many of Leskov's earlier writings) and by describing in detail Figura's encounter with Count Osten-Saken, his divisional commander. He does manage to capture the peculiarly Russian piety of the count who, in spite of his rigid adherence to the forms of conventional religion, is able to admire Figura's high moral standards. But, on the whole, Figura is portrayed as far too virtuous a character to come fully to life. Leskov sought Tolstoy's advice on the story, and clearly wrote it having in mind such Tolstoyan tenets as nonviolence, vegetarianism, and living by one's own labor.

"Chelovek na chasakh" (The Sentry, 1887) exists to confound critics who describe Leskov as a verbose writer who paid insufficient attention to form. It is a taut, economically constructed story whose short chapters, each devoted to a single incident, rush along with Pushkinian dynamism and sense of inevitability. Once again, Leskov draws upon an actual event from the reign of Nicholas I and manages to reproduce the feel of the era, with its iron discipline and heartless bureaucracy. During the winter of 1839 a sudden thaw weakens the ice on the Neva River in St. Petersburg. Postnikov, "a very nervous and sensitive" private soldier, is standing sentry duty outside the Winter Palace when he hears the cries of a man floundering about on the ice. It is late at night and no one else is about; Postnikov knows that the man will surely drown if no one rescues him but he also knows that flogging and exile, perhaps even the firing squad, await a sentry who deserts his post. But he listens to his conscience and is pulling the man to shore when an officer drives past and, quickly sizing up the situation, decides to take credit for saving the drowning man. Postnikov cannot hide his temporary desertion and is immediately arrested.

Thus far the story is a fairly straightforward account of a moral dilemma, but Leskov then skillfully transforms it into a biting satire against institutional morality. The focus shifts away from Postnikov to the motives of the others involved in the affair. The officer who claims credit for the rescue simply wishes to satisfy his vanity, hoping to receive a medal for lifesaving. Lieutenant-Colonel Svinin, Postnikov's commanding officer, wishes to cover up the affair to keep his service record unstained. Kokoshkin, the Chief of Police, is concerned to keep the tsar from learning of the sentry's desertion. Kokoshkin manages to achieve his end by accepting the clearly false claim of the officer; the officer gets his medal and is satisfied; Svinin's record is left unstained and so he too is satisfied. Yet, Svinin feels, there is at least one loose end: Postnikov has committed a serious breach of military discipline and must be punished. Thus ultimately even Postnikov is "satisfied" with the 200 strokes of the birch he receives: he had expected much worse. The sharpest barb of all is inserted at the very end of the story. Svinin recounts the whole affair to a highly placed personage in the church (a figure not identified, but clearly modeled on Metropolitan Filaret of Moscow, whom Leskov despised). Svinin has thus far been cast as the major villain of the story, but even he feels a twinge of conscience over punishing Postnikov, who has, after all, risked his own life to save another's. But the Metropolitan, in a series of trite and utterly heartless phrases, assures him that one must always do one's duty, that corporal punishment is fully accord with the Holy Scriptures, and that the whole affair must remain a secret. "Evidently," Leskov concludes, "the Metropolitan too was satisfied" (8.173). The fact that all concerned in the affair are satisfied at its "happy ending," wherein virtue has not only gone unrewarded but been severely punished, is a vivid illustration of the power of institutions to obscure elementary humanity. "The Sentry" is a good example of Leskov's art, through which a simple anecdote becomes a powerful story and in which his moral point is stated most skillfully. Here too, the pointed contrast between Postnikov's instinctive humanity and the heartlessness of the "system" owes much to the influence of Tolstoy.

Leskov was very proud of his righteous men, and considered them one of his major contributions to Russian literature. As he told his biographer Faresov, "the strength of my talent is in positive types . . . . Show me another writer who has such an abundance of positive Russian types."[3] Contemporary judgment may not place as high a value on his righteous men as did Leskov, yet it cannot be denied that he achieved the difficult feat of creating many characters who are both good and credible. So much virtue taken together, can, of course, easily become cloying, and Leskov is most successful when he conveys the color and originality of his characters instead of concentrating solely on their virtues. The reason for Leskov's pride in this cycle of stories is ultimately an extraliterary one. He wished to show the day-to-day working of a system of ethics which sprang from Christianity but which often had little in common with the church. Indeed, the moral feat (*podvig*) of the righteous man consists in following the dictates of his conscience even when they conflict with conventional morality. This conflict becomes sharper and more explicit in those stories written after 1885, when Leskov became increasingly caught up with Tolstoy's teachings. The fact that his righteous men most often come from professions which have their own rigid system of ethics (the police, the bureaucracy, the army) makes such conflict inevitable.

The remoteness of most of the righteous men as individuals is doubtless necessary. They are intended to have something of the function of icons: colorful, unique, perhaps even inspiring, but purged of human failings. Close inner scrutiny would inevitably reveal their flaws and diminish their virtues. The colorful surface would crack if they began to breathe.

II   *Legends and Folktales*

The positive ideal in Leskov's writings found expression in the later 1880's in a series of legends set in the early centuries of Christianity which he adapted from stories found in the Russian *Prolog*.[4] The *Prolog*, a compendium of brief saints' lives, sermons, moralistic anecdotes, and other edifying reading arranged for each day of the year, was itself originally translated from the Greek in the early twelfth century and enlarged over the years with additional Slavic material. It was perhaps the single most popular item of reading matter of medieval Russia and later provided inspiration for writers such as Pushkin, Dostoevsky, and Tolstoy.

Leskov explains some of his motivations for turning to the *Prolog* in his comments to the first legend he published, "Luchshii Bogomolets" (The Best Implorer of God, 1886). Two related themes — his polemic with the church and his increasing admiration for Tolstoy's moral-religious stance — run through his comments. He begins by defending Tolstoy against those who attacked him for supposedly harmful tendencies in his moralistic fables of the 1880s, some of which were based on the *Prolog*. One need only examine Tolstoy's sources, Leskov states, to see that his stories are in fact beneficial since they originate in material fully in the spirit of popular religious beliefs and considered edifying by the church. But his real motivations are by no means as innocent as would appear. The tale he retells — about a woodcutter who lives a life of utter simplicity and poverty but whose prayers prove more efficacious that those of a bishop — suggests that people outside the church or only marginally attached to it may possess a stronger faith than its most respected representatives. This story, like most of the later ones, continues Leskov's polemic with official religion by demonstrating that the church is not a requisite for a virtuous life. He attempts to undermine the importance of the church by showing individuals who have fashioned their own system of ethics based on the original sources of Christianity rather than on what the church has added. By moving closer to the sources of Christianity he makes the discrepancy between the simple faith of his protagonists and the ossified dogmatism of the official church all the more glaring. Leskov is thus doing here what he had so often done before — using material from another age (in this case, material officially sanctioned by the church) to take issue with his own.

Criticism of established religion is at the center of "Skazanie o Fedor-khristianine i o druge ego Abrame-zhidovine" (The Legend of Fedor the Christian and his Friend Avram the Hebrew, 1886), based on the *Prolog* tale of October 31. A Christian family and a Jewish family live together in friendship in a pagan Byzantium, respecting each other's faiths. But as Christianity becomes the official religion, the church claims a monopoly on truth and preaches intolerance and enmity toward other religions. Fedor and Avram, remembering their childhood friendship, manage to transcend religious prejudice, and Avram saves his friend from financial ruin. At the story's end they join forces to build a refuge for children of all faiths. The story is clearly directed against religious and racial prejudice (the pogroms of the early 1880s had not yet faded from memory) and helps compensate for some of Leskov's earlier anti-Semitic writings. But in spite of its admirable ecumenical sentiments, it has little distinction as a work of art. It is sentimentalized and saccharine, and its moral lesson emerges far too obviously because of the totally black and white shades in which the characters are drawn. The style is simplified to the point of dullness, and the highly colored setting which lends some charm to later legends is missing here.

"Skomorokh Pamfalon" (Pamfalon the Buffoon, 1887) is among Leskov's better *Prolog* tales, one which closely follows the pattern of his "righteous men" in that its central figure devotes himself to a life of active love toward his fellows. Ermy, a man of wealth and power in fourth-century Byzantium, finds it impossible to adhere to his Chistian beliefs amid the luxury and hypocrisy around him and resolves to save his soul by living a sinless life. He gives away his wealth and retreats to the desert where he spends thirty years sitting on a rocky pillar, living on the offerings of the faithful and despairing because only he will be worthy of salvation. One day he hears a voice commanding him to go to Damascus and seek out a truly worthy man, Pamfalon. Ermy is shocked to find that Pamfalon is a professional buffoon who spends his days entertaining the dissolute. He learns that Pamfalon, too, has wanted to retreat from the city to devote himself to the salvation of his soul, but has used the money which would have enabled him to give up his profession to save a woman in desperate need. Ermy returns to the desert comforted that he will not be alone in eternity only to find that a flock of birds has nested in his pillar. "That is as it should be," he says. "Birds should live among the crags and man should serve men" (8.230). He abandons his quest for self-perfection and becomes a herdsman and teacher for nearby villagers.

Leskov has changed the original *Prolog* source (December 3) considerably, adding a good deal of historical detail and color and significantly altering the point of the story. In the original, the hermit does not reject the contemplative life outright, but returns to his pillar marveling that good men are to be found everywhere. Although Leskov's *Prolog* stories are generally written in harmony with Tolstoy's teachings, this one and others contain signs that Leskov was not an uncritical disciple. Pamfalon, for instance, remarks that the woman he saved would not have needed help had Ermy remained in office, since he could easily have prevented such an injustice — a very un-Tolstoyan argument for the necessity of worldly power.

"Sovestnyi Danila" (Conscience-stricken Danila, 1888), under June 7 in the *Prolog*, clearly shows the tension between Leskov's impulse to tell an exciting story and his desire to create a simple, moralistic fable, a tension which runs through most of the later stories of the cycle as well. Like "Pamfalon," it concerns a man who finds that he must go outside the church to find salvation. Danila, a holy hermit, is enslaved by a band of pagan nomads but manages to kill his captors and flee. This act of murder troubles his conscience, so he visits the patriarchs of the church, and even the Pope himself, to ask for guidance. They all assure him that killing a barbarian does not conflict with Christian teachings, but none can show him a passage in scripture that would justify murder. Only at the end of his life does he realize that "the conscience which oppressed him must in truth be considered not the punishment of an implacable God but a good reminder which would not allow [him] to lull himself into complacency" (PSS, 30.18). He realizes that he must accept full responsibility for his crime and attempt to atone for it by devoting the rest of his life to serving others.

The first half of the story — Danila's captivity and escape — is exciting and full of naturalistic detail (it recalls "The Enchanted

Pilgrim'' is this regard, as well as in theme), but the second half is simply dull. Here Leskov must treat in detail a state of mind — Danila's guilty conscience — something which his talents poorly equipped him to do. Danila's sudden revelation of the function of conscience, for example, is unconvincing because it is abrupt and unmotivated. Leskov tries to do too much in one brief story: to re-affirm the Tolstoyan view of the evil of any killing; to puncture the complacency of a church which would justify killing; to examine the role of conscience; and to affirm a Christianity based on active love and service to others.

"Lev startsa Gerasima" (The Lion of the Elder Gerasim, 1888) found under March 4 in the *Prolog*, also illustrates a Tolstoyan tenet — nonviolent resistance to evil — but the story is a slight piece of work, and Leskov's attempt to write it in a simplified, "Tol-stoyan" manner falls flat. "Prekrasnaia Aza" (Beautiful Aza, 1888), on the other hand, was much praised by Leskov's contem-poraries, and he took great pains in writing it, complaining of the torments he suffered while polishing the style. Aza, a young Egyp-tian girl, sells all her possessions in order to pay a certain man's debts and so save him for suicide. She herself is reduced to poverty and becomes a prostitute in order to survive. When she learns of Christ's teachings she resolves to become a Christian herself, but the priests insist that she must first repent of her past sins, fast, and study the dogmas of the church. She dies before she can be for-mally accepted into the faith but a miracle occurs when two angels descend to bear her soul into Heaven. Leskov's considerable modifications of the original source ("The Tale of the Maiden," April 8) are revealing. He adds a characteristic dash of piquancy: the man whom Aza saves has a daughter whom his creditor lusts after, offering to cancel the debt in exchange for the girl. The miraculous element, so important in the original, is considerably played down. The attacks on the formalism of the church are, of course, Leskov's additions. The excessive sentimentality of the story was perhaps the very quality which appealed to Leskov's con-temporary reader, who was captivated by myths of the noble prostitute.

"Askalonskii zlodei" (The Brigand of Askalon, 1889) is a highly embroidered version of "The Tale of the Merchant" under June 14 in the *Prolog*. Leskov's account has some moments of high drama, but these are all but lost amid the bathos and welter of improbable incidents. Falaley, a rich merchant and shipowner, loses all his ships in a catastrophe and is imprisoned for debts. Miliya, a high-ranking official, comes to Askalon to pass judgment on a vicious criminal, Anastas, and is smitten by Teniya, Falaley's beautiful pagan wife. Miliya offers to pay Falaley's debts if Teniya will agree to spend a night with him, but she vows to remain faithful to her husband. Leskov pulls out all the stops in describing the incredible pressure put on Teniya to submit (the larger part of the story is a veritable "Perils of Pauline"), but Teniya staunchly resists the advances of the archvillain Miliya. Her devotion to her husband softens the heart of the brigand Anastas (although the representatives of official Christianity have remained unmoved), and he tells her where to find gold he has buried so that she can ransom her husband. Ultimately virtue triumphs as the villains are dispatched and Teniya leads her dazed husband off to bed. Leskov revels in excessively painful details, and his description of "Herod's prison" is a catalogue of horrors, all of which, he insisted, he had collected from various *Prolog* accounts. Leskov's macabre humor, which enlivens many of his other works, is highly inappropriate here, and undermines any moral point he may have hoped to make in the story. For example, at one point Teniya decides that she must seek advice from a purportedly prophetic skull which lies in the town cemetery. On her way there she encounters two members of Anastas' robber band who tell her that they have been searching for money buried under the skull but were unable to move it by twisting and tugging and even tearing off strips of skin which still adhered to it. When they noticed that the skull appeared to be staring at them, they fled in terror. Teniya persists and find that it is not a skull but the head of a holy hermit, very much alive, who has buried himself up to the neck and who refused to break his vow of silence even while the robbers were tearing off his ears! Then too, the story's style is hyperbolic: "Teniya stood listening, tensed like a resilient bow, and scarcely had Anastas uttered his last word to her when she sprang away like an arrow from the bowstring and flew off in the direction of Azot" (PSS, 30.81).

"Gora" (The Mountain, 1890, originally titled "Zenon, the Goldsmith") is another of the better *Prolog*-based stories, but is marred by some of the same flaws as "The Brigand of Askalon." Nefora, an Egyptian beauty, conceives a passion for Zenon, a Christian goldsmith famous in Alexandria. When Zenon feels he might succumb to Nefora's charms, he seizes a dagger and puts out his own eye. She then resolves to seek vengeance against him and against the faith for which he has rejected her. It happens that the Nile is late in flooding and the people of the city, threatened with starvation, are restless. Nefora persuades Alexandria's ruler to use the Christains as scapegoats: he demands that they prove their faith by praying that a mountain will move to dam the Nile and flood the fields. If they fail they will be put to death. The leading Christians all flee the city when they learn of this, and Zenon, although not regarded as a Christian by the church, is summoned because his faith has been proven when he put out his eye. Zenon prays, and in fact a violent rainstorm floods the river and part of the mountain crumbles away. Nefora, moved by Zenon's faith, is totally reformed, and becomes his wife.

On this occasion, Leskov's additions to the original *Prolog* source (October 7) are appropriate. The plot of the work is particularly well constructed, and the events thoroughly motivated. The detailed descriptions of life in Alexandria are saturated with color and apt detail, and reveal Leskov's extensive research (as well as his borrowings from the novels of the German Egyptologist Georg Ebers). He again agonized over the style of the work: " 'The Mountain' was rewritten so many times that I lost count, and so it is true that the style in places attains the quality of music" (11.460). But here, as in other stories, he fails to solve the problem of creating dialogue which would sound solemn and antique without being stilted. The story's ending also reveals a weakness of most of Leskov's *Prolog* tales. He wishes to play down the "miraculous" moving of the mountain and to show that the real miracle wrought by Zenon's faith is Nefora's conversion from a purely sensual passion to a higher form of universal love and willingness for self-sacrifice. Although Leskov provides a sound enough explanation for the moving of the mountain, Nefora's sudden change of faith is unconvincing. The purely physical, the surface of things, was Leskov's province; when dealing with subtle spiritual processes he can do little more than follow the laconic remarks of the prototype stories. The result is an unbalanced effort, with some extremely vivid accounts of the surface of life but with unconvincing characters. Thus it is that we have a fascinating and full-blooded description of Nefora's attempted seduction of Zenon, while his "moral victory" over his passion — by far the more important if Leskov really is trying to point out a moral — is given short shrift.

The tension between implicit meaning and explicit moral present in many *Prolog* tales is stronger in "Nevinnyi Prudentsyi"

(Innocent Prudentsy, 1891), the last story of the cycle. A lengthy
and quite pointless introduction, tedious dialogues, and clumsy
plot construction make this one of the weakest works of the cycle,
and yet it deserves comment for what it reveals about Leskov's Tolstoyan beliefs. The kernel of the story is a brief anecdote describing
how Melita, a beautiful young widow who has dedicated her life to
the highest of Christian ideals, cures Prudentsy of his apparently
all-consuming passion for her. She takes him and a slave girl to an
uninhabited island where she makes him agree to spend three days
alone in a cave with no food. When the three days have elapsed
Prudentsy has lost all interest in the marriage bed. She abandons
him and the slave girl Marema on the island, and a year later Prudentsy is the father of robust twins. Prudentsy then sums up, incredibly, the "moral" of the story: "We must consider the spirit and
not the flesh to be the master of life and must not live for those feelings which lead us to separate ourselves from all other people"
(9.115). Yet everything in Prudentsy's experience suggests quite the
contrary: the demands of the flesh proved stronger than his love for
Melita, and his joyously sensual life on the island with Marema,
"separated from all other people," has suited him admirably. The
happy ending — the last scene is an apotheosis of the family, with
Marema contentedly breast-feeding her children — is far from the
ideal of selfless dedication which Melita aims for. The story thus
implicitly affirms the more mundane value of simple family life,
and suggests that Melita's ideal is simply too lofty to be attained by
more than a few saints. As Prudentsy admits, "Her spirit is too elevated and serious; it too mercilessly [sic] vanquishes the flesh"
(9.115).

"Bramadata i Radovan" (Bramadata and Radovan: An Indian
Legend) does not originate in the *Prolog*, although is is similar to
the other legends. Also similar is the jarring discrepancy between
the events in the story and the superimposed moral. It purports to
illustrate Tolstoy's doctrine of nonviolent resistance, but fails to
convince. Bramadata, a warlike Indian King, invades the kingdom
of Radovan, a man of peace, and puts him to death. Radovan's
son, Dolgozhiv, is spared, and eventually, his real identity unknown, becomes Bramadata's trusted servant. When at last he
finds himself alone with Bramadata, he seizes him and prepares to
cut his throat. Bramadata pleads for his life and repents of his past.
Dolgozhiv remembers the last words of his father, "Enmity is
softened not by enmity but by meekness," and spares him. But the

story scarcely illustrates this moral: Radovan's unwillingness to resist evil costs him his life; Bramadata is not reformed through
meekness but by the sheer terror of the sword poised over his
throat. If Leskov could write of nonviolence with no more conviction than this, his faith must have been weak indeed.

III   *Didactic Stories*

Also in the matrix of Tolstoyan Christianity are a number of
short didactic tales, some of which were published in *Posrednik*
(The Intermediary). These, like Tolstoy's own, are modeled on
folktales and are written in the language of the people. The first,
"Malan'ia-golova baran'ia" (Malanya Muttonhead, 1888), is also
the best. It recounts how the selfless love of an old peasant woman,
whom everyone considers a fool because she thinks more of others
than of herself, manages to defeat even Death himself. The tale is
written in simple yet very artful language, with racy dialogue full of
proverbs and colorful expressions. "Durachok" (The Little Fool,
1891) is a children's story also about a person whose goodness convinces those around him that he is a fool. Only the "heathen"
Tatars finally recognize that he is indeed a righteous man. "Pusto-
pliasy" (1893) is cast as a Christmas story and concerns the
peasants of a village who lose all after they refuse to share their
grain with their famine-stricken neighbors. It is told in a most cir-
cumstantial manner by a peasant narrator, and its point — active
concern for the sufferings of others — emerges almost in the form
of a threat. "Khristos v gostiakh u muzhika" (Christ Visits a
Peasant, 1881) is similar in theme to Tolstoy's "God Sees the Truth
but Waits" but vastly different in manner. Tolstoy's story is a
simple but moving account of a man unjustly accused of a crime
who nonetheless forgives the real culprit. Leskov's version is sentimentalized and is told in an elaborate manner full of extraneous incident which dilutes its essentially simple moral.

But the contrast between Leskov's manner and Tolstoy's is most
evident in another pair of stories. Leskov's "Chas voli Bozhiei"
(The Hour of God's Will, 1890) was based on an idea suggested by
Tolstoy. A king is told by a wise man that his kingdom is not flour-
ishing because he does not know what time is the most important,
what man is the most important, and what action is the most important.
He asks other wise men, but finally it is a young girl who answers:
"The time is now, this very minute; the man is the one you are now

with, and the action is the one done to save your soul."[5] Tolstoy
was unhappy with Leskov's treatment of his theme and wrote his
own version, "Three Questions," in 1903. Tolstoy's four-page story
achieves its power through the utter simplicity of its style, stripped
of imagery and effects, and its total concentration on its moral
point. Leskov's runs to twenty-seven pages and is written in a play-
ful *skaz*-fashion with stylistic fireworks rivaling those of "Lefty";
its moral point is all but lost amid hyperbole and farcical incident.
A comparison of a similar incident from each makes the point
clear, and also reveals something about Leskov's Tolstoyanism. In
both stories the king seeks a holy hermit to answer the questions.
Tolstoy's king goes to the hermit himself and finds him digging in
his garden: "He greeted the king when he saw him and at once set
to digging again. The hermit was thin and weak and he breathed
heavily as he dug the spade in the ground and turned over small
lumps of earth."[6] Leskov's king, on the other hand, grandly sends
out "fifty emissaries in all directions," each equipped with "bas-
kets woven out of soft straw, the kind geese are carried in to fight
on the ice before the royal chambers. And the king commanded the
bottom of each basket to be packed with odorous hay and soft,
stringy moss from an old pine tree, and on top of this to be
sprinkled just a bit of down and plucked feathers, so as to have
something to pack the hermits in" (9.9). Leskov's king learns of
not one but three righteous men in his kingdom who live as holy
hermits:

> One of them, the eldest, let his light shine in the very wildest and thickest
> part of the forest where he had long ago climbed up in an oak tree, right to
> the very tip, and now the oak had grown up tall and bumped against the
> heavens. And the sun roasts this saintly old man and the winds buffet him.
> His name is Dubovik and his age is well over a thousand years. The second
> old fellow — this is the middle brother to the first — flourished in the
> boundless steppe amid the feather-grass that grows so tall it covers the
> cranes and bustards right up to their heads and could hide an armored
> warrior and his lance. The old fellow has buried himself in the earth to the
> waist and endures the earthworm gnawing at him, while he himself feeds
> only on tiny insects that happen to crawl into his mouth. And the name of
> this hermit is Polevik and his age is five hundred. The third old man — the
> youngest brother of the first two — stands up to his very neck in the mid-
> dle of impenetrable swamps where he lives with the frogs and snakes and
> the gadfly stings his face and the whining mosquito has already sucked all
> of the blood out of him, but the old man still stands, never stirring. His

name is Vodovik and his age is three hundred, less a year. And all these amazing holy men are now barely alive so that one must handle them with great caution and care, because with only the very slightest jolt all of them could crumble to pieces." (9.9)

The story continues to pile up extravagant incidents until almost the end, when the questions are answered and the moral stated. But this sudden shift to a serious note, coming after pages of delightful whimsy, is particularly jarring, and the moral point quite inappropriate in the context of the story as a whole. Tolstoy, who judged the story on the basis of its moral worth, complained of Leskov's "particular shortcoming which, it would seem, could be so easily corrected and which in itself is a positive quality and not a shortcoming — an *exubérance* of images, colors, distinctive expressions which intoxicate and fascinate. There is much that is unnecessary and disproportionate, but the verve and tone are marvelous. Still, the tale is a good one, but it is annoying that it could have been better were it not for an excess of talent."[7] Intoxicated by the color and language of the story, the reader can scarcely take its "message" seriously. Leskov's story may be a failure as a didactic work, but its stylistic brilliance and sheer inventiveness make it a delight to read.

Two other stories of the period are not cast as folktales but are indicative of Leskov's desire to engage in Tolstoyan didacticism. "Tomlenie dukha" (Languor of the Spirit, 1890) is a children's story illustrating the harm of swearing oaths, written in a sentimental and unconvincing manner and filled with cheerless moralizing. "Pod Rozhdestvo obideli" (Offended before Christmas, 1890) relates several anecdotes concerning robberies at Christmas time and questions the propriety of judging others. It is written in a simple, conversational style addressed directly to the reader, which here is appropriate and effective.

Not many of Leskov's *Prolog* tales and didactic stories can be numbered among his finest creations. Their popularity in Leskov's lifetime is no doubt due to the then current vogue for antiquity and the keen interest in Tolstoy's philosophy and moral and religious questions generally. To fashion them he was forced to try to keep in check one of the finest and strongest of his talents — his keen sense of irony. At their best, the stories of this cycle contain scenes of vivid color, exciting incident, and absorbing narrative; at their worst, they show that curious blend of coy eroticism, gratuitous

violence, and sentimental piety familiar from the cheaper Holly-
wood Biblical epics. Two impulses — to entertain and to state a
moral — seldom exist in harmony here. Another major problem
arises from the clash of conventions. What may be appropriate and
acceptable in the original *Prolog* stories, with their laconic style of
narrative and their acceptance of the miraculous as a fact of everyday life, cannot be so readily transferred into a work written with
the detailed descriptions, dialogue, and psychological motivation
characteristic of nineteenth-century realism.

The *Prolog* tales and other stories reveal that Leskov was not an
uncritical disciple of Tolstoy the artist nor of Tolstoy the religious
thinker. His attempts to write in a Tolstoyan manner are not successful. As he himself admitted to Chertkov, "To write in as simple
a manner as Lev Nikolaevich is beyond my capability. It is not
among my talents.... I have grown accustomed to adorning my
works and cannot write more simply." (11.369). He is at his best
when he abandons simplicity in favor of his own ornate manner.
Likewise, Tolstoy's ascetic ideal is scarcely Leskov's. He gives full
due to the life of the senses, and when he strives to deny it, he does
so with little conviction. As "Prudentsy" shows, however much
Leskov may have admired that chilly ideal, he was well aware that
it was a remote one to which only a few could aspire. The formula-
tion of a positive ideal in Leskov's fiction was encouraged, but not
fundamentally altered, by his encounter with Tolstoy's ideas. The
righteous men of the 1880s and 1890s are essentially those of the
1870s: honest men and women whose conscience leads them to
transcend the self by serving others.

CHAPTER 6

Occasional Pieces and Satires

I *Christmas Stories*

I N the 1880's Leskov wrote a series of Christmas stories which he
published in a separate collection in 1886 and again assembled as
a group for his *Collected Works.*[1] Such stories were traditional in
popular magazines of the age and had some very distinctive traits.
One of Leskov's characters provides a good description when he
complains of the difficulty of producing an original Christmas
story which would meet all the requirements of the genre: "It is a
type of literature in which the writer is a prisoner of an excessively
narrow and rigidly defined form. A Christmas story must without
fail be set on an evening of the Christmas season—between Christmas Day and Epiphany; there must be an element of the supernatural; it must have some sort of moral, even if it only consists in
dispelling some harmful prejudice; and finally, it must absolutely
have a happy ending." (7.433). Although some of Leskov's Christmas stories do conform to these specifications, it is clear that he
attempts to expand the possibilities of the genre. This he does by
mocking its conventions: the "supernatural" is always shown to
have a rational explanation; the happy ending may be highly ironic;
the moral is often quite surprising. Some stories make no pretense
to any supernatural element: as Leskov said in the foreword to the
1886 edition, the astonishing qualities of Russian society and the
Russian spirit can themselves provide enough of the fantastic and
enigmatic.

The first of the series, "Belyi orel" (The White Eagle, 1880) is an
absorbing, if somewhat improbable "ghost story" told by a high-
ranking bureaucrat, Galaktion Ilich. He was once sent incognito by
the Minister of Justice, Count Panin, to investigate rumors of ad-

ministrative abuses by a provincial governor. Panin promises that
Galaktion will receive a coveted decoration, the White Eagle, for
his services. In the provincial capital he is assigned a secretary, a
young man of strikingly good looks and vitality with the odd name
of Akvilyalbov (Russified form of the Latin *aquila alba*— "white
eagle"). Akvilyalbov, a popular member of town society because
of his fine talent as an amateur actor and musician, dies
mysteriously and suddenly, and a rumor quickly spreads that
Galaktion has given him the evil eye. Galaktion himself admits that
his skeletal appearance frightens those who first meet him.
Thereafter Galaktion is convinced that he sees the dead clerk
following him everywhere and becomes so unnerved that he cannot
carry out a thorough investigation. On his return to St. Petersburg
he does not receive the expected decoration, but Akvilyalbov's
visits cease. Three years later, when the original incipient scandal in
the provinces has been forgotten, Akvilyalbov appears again, this
time to deliver the promised "White Eagle."

It might appear initially that this is but a farfetched ghost story
designed only to aid the digestion of Christmas dinner, but Leskov
drops more than a few hints that the only evil spirits at work are
ones clothed in flesh and blood, and that the real matter of the
story is a highly organized conspiracy in which Galaktion is
thoroughly duped.[2] The story is framed, and the first narrator
suggests that stories of the supernatural are usually highly colored
by the fantasies of those who tell them. Galaktion himself is
portrayed as a dreamer and a man of lively imagination. Akvilyalbov (a name no doubt chosen by the conspirators to mock Galaktion) is an actor of sufficient talent to
be able to feign death and later convince Galaktion—who cannot
but help feel some guilt for the "death" of his secretary—that he is
indeed being visited by a ghost. Thus the story is really an exposé of
how the provincial governor and the minister of justice himself
have used Galaktion to frustrate a thorough inquiry into their
corrupt dealings. "The White Eagle" does follow most of the
conventions of the Christmas story genre: the holiday setting
(decorations were awarded at New Year's); the happy ending
(Galaktion is rewarded for allowing the conspirators to continue
their crimes); and even a moral, which one might sum up as "One
sees only so much as he would like to see," or, in the words of the
epigraph, "The dog dreams of bread, the fisherman of fish."

A masterfully told story, also based on a brief anecdote, is

"Prividenie v Inzhenernom zamke" (The Apparition in the Engineers' Castle, 1882). This, too, is a ghost story without a ghost, but one does not know until the very last page that the frightful apparition is flesh and blood. The story is set in the St. Petersburg "Engineers' Castle," reputed to be haunted even before Tsar Paul I was murdered in it in 1801. The cadets in the Engineering School later housed there were well aware of the building's reputation, and delighted in frightening one another with tales of spirits and apparitions. When the school's despised director dies the cadets cannot help but feel relieved, but are warned by their priest that their conscience, "the man in gray," will visit them if they rejoice in the death of another. Under such circumstances four cadets are detailed to stand watch over the coffin while all the others are away attending a memorial service. When the cadet who suffered most from the harshness of the director decides to pull the nose of the corpse in a show of bravado, he is terrified to hear the corpse apparently sigh, and petrified when he sees a gray figure slowly move across the room to kiss the corpse in the coffin.

The seemingly fantastic events are convincingly explained: the "apparition" was the director's ill and grief-stricken wife who came to say one last farewell to her husband. The story is exceptionally well constructed and the cadets' behavior fully motivated. There is even a moral neatly illustrated by the events and stated unobtrusively by the priest: he tells the cadets, "there is someone who loves and takes pity on every man." "The Apparition in the Engineer's Castle" is one of Leskov's finest Christmas stories, and a model of its kind.

"Zver'" (The Beast, 1883) illustrates both the strong points and the weaknesses of Christmas stories: on the one hand, it is absorbing and entertaining; on the other, it is marred by a sentimental and utterly unconvincing ending. Written as a recollection from Leskov's own childhood, the story describes a capriciously cruel landowner (loosely modeled on Leskov's uncle Strakhov) who keeps bear cubs and releases them for hunting when they become vicious. Khraposhka, the serf who looks after the bears, grows to love one particularly intelligent bear called Sganarelle. Sganarelle is to be released for a hunt on Christmas Day and the uncle, learning of Khraposhka's unwillingness to harm the beast, deliberately assigns him as one of the marksmen who is to shoot him. Sganarelle manages to escape in a dramatic and highly original fashion and the uncle is furious. The whole household waits in trepidation for an explosion of the uncle's wrath but he, on hearing the local priest explaining the words of a Christmas carol to the children, is moved to tears and completely transformed. He gives Khraposhka his freedom and spends the rest of his life helping the poor. This sudden and scarcely motivated reformation of the uncle unfortunately spoils what is otherwise a fine story. Leskov sacrifices veracity to the demands of the genre for a moral and a happy ending. When one compares, say, Dickens's treatment of a similar theme, the flaws in Leskov's story become all the more evident.

Several of the stories in the collection are reminiscent of the young Chekhov (indeed his "In the Bath-House" is a variation on Leskov's "Puteshestvie s nigilistom" [A Journey with a Nihilist, 1882]). And the resemblance is not accidental: with the rapid expansion of literacy in the late 1870's and early 1880's, a new market was created for amusing, short, and essentially short-lived fiction. Both Chekhov and Leskov published in the newspapers and new mass-circulation weeklies such as *Oskolki* (Fragments), which catered to the demands of these new readers for entertaining reading. Leskov's "Shtopal'shchik" (The Mender, 1882), "Malen'kaia oshibka" (A Slight Error, 1883) and "Dukh gospozhi Zhanlis" (The Spirit of Mme. de Genlis, 1881) are fine examples of what the market demanded — mildly satirical and skillfully told anecdotes.

The tendency of the mass-market story to adapt itself to popular tastes is at least one factor which led Leskov to include in his collection two stories with some anti-Semitic elements. Anti-Semitism increased in the late 1870's, boiling over in the pogroms of the spring of 1881, and popular periodicals of the day often found cheap and crude sources of humor in mockery of the Jews. Leskov's stories are both framed, and the narrators are army officers, a group perhaps more inclined to anti-Semitism than the average Russian. Although the ridicule of the Jews is attributed to the narrator rather than to Leskov himself, there is little doubt that he gave way to his own anti-Jewish feelings here. To be sure, Leskov often manages to make his Russians appear as absurd as his Jews. But even the colorful incidents and lively language of "Zhidovskaia kuvyrkalegiia" (Jewish Somersault, 1882) dealing with the attempts of Jews to avoid military service, cannot mask its distasteful anti-Semitic flavor. "Obman" (Deception, 1883) also deals with the allegedly crafty nature of the Jews. What in itself is a none-too-clever anecdote is spun out to great length by the inclusion of much peripheral incident. A third related story (not included in the Christmas cycle) illustrates Leskov's predilection for puzzling titles. "Rakushanskii melamed" (The Melamed of Rakousko, 1878 ["Melamed" — a teacher of Hebrew and religion in a Jewish school; "Rakousko"— Czech name for Austria] allows Leskov to display his detailed knowledge of Jewish religious beliefs and customs. Here again the basis is a rather simple anecdote of how a servant girl proved herself to be wiser than a learned melamed, but the effect is marred by some cheap humor at the expense of the Jews.

"Grabezh" (A Case of Robbery) was originally published as a Christmas story in 1887, but not included in the cycle. A summary can scarcely do justice to the manner in which Leskov's narrative talents transform a tired device of mistaken identity into comic masterpiece. The setting — Leskov's Orel — is sketched with fond detail and obvious authority. The suffocating atmosphere of provincial merchant life and its conventional piety, an overbearing mother determined to protect her strapping son against the realities of life, and some fine genre pictures (the singing contest to select a new deacon is a gem) all build up to a farcical climax — a comic battle in the darkness during which the narrator and his uncle, terrified of the town's legendary felons, find that they themselves are the robbers. Even better is the language of the story, both dialogue and narration. Leskov was on familiar ground in reproducing the full flavor of the spoken language of his native city.

Leskov's Christmas stories are thus an uneven lot: there are a number of gems, but many suffer from a flaw inherent in the genre itself. They were written for a specific occasion, intended to be read once and forgotten. The excessive sentimentality of some and the anti-Semitism of others are partly attributable to the journalistic milieu in which they appeared. The level of taste of the newly established mass-circulation periodicals tended to sink to that of the lowest common denominator, and Leskov was not always successful in resisting this tendency. Yet he does manage (in "The White Eagle," "The Apparition in the Engineers' Castle," and "A Case of Robbery") to produce works which, although written within the narrow confines of the genre, are a delight to read not only at Christmas but at any time of any year.

II *Stories "À Propos"*

A second cycle, published as "Stories *À Propos"* in 1887, also
grew out of Leskov's journalism of the 1880s. Like his Christmas
stories, these are a mixed lot. Leskov himself described them as
"journal feuilletons . . . ordinary stories, not out of the common
run, but no worse than those which are fussed over as something
exceptional" (11. 343). The common factor is supposedly some
contemporary event which the narrator comments upon by recal-
ling an incident from the past or producing an old but relevant
document. Leskov was fond of using memoirs or old manuscripts
to enable him to make oblique comments on the events of the day.[3]
But the connection with contemporary affairs is often very vague,
and his motive is as much to entertain as it is to comment. As a narrator of one story remarks about what he has just related, "There
are no ideas in it which are worth anything; I told it simply for its
interest's sake" (8. 111)

"Sovmestiteli" (The Pluralists, 1884) is an amusing story which
was no doubt as *à propos* in the 1880's as in the 1840's, when it
supposedly occurred. Leskov explains that wealthy and powerful
men of that era were expected to keep a mistress: Count Kankrin,
Minister of Finance for Nicholas I, conformed to the custom. But
the count was an old and very busy man who, as Leskov notes slyly,
kept his mistress "simply for the sake of decency." His mistress
naturally enough demands attention, and the count decides to
follow another practice of the time and engage a young man of suitable background and manners — a "pluralist"— who could cater
to the needs of the restive mistress. But before Kankrin can do this,
he finds that his mistress already has a lover who happens to be a
junior functionary in Kankrin's own ministry. Kankrin is relieved
when he arranges to marry the two off, but his plan backfires: his
former mistress proves most adroit at exploiting the system of
favoritism and bribery on which the bureaucracy rests, and he can
only watch the meteoric rise of the pluralist's career with increasing
apprehension. Kankrin is finally forced to arrange the young man's
transfer to a different ministry. It is a lively story with many satirical jibes at the bureaucratic practices of the 1840's and, by infer-
ence, at those same practices in the 1880's.

"Interesnye muzhchiny" (Interesting Men, 1885) is indeed one
of the most interesting stories in the collection, though unfortunately marred by some very obvious defects. It is told by an

old cavalry officer *à propos* of a remark that there are no longer any "interesting men" left. The narrator describes an incident from his youth when his regiment was stationed in a provincial town and the officers passed their time in the traditional military fashion, with wine, women, and cards. A Polish civilian, Avgust Matveich, joins them for an evening of cards. He loses heavily, then announces that 12,000 rubles he carried in his waistcoat are missing. The officers, stung by what seems to be a slur on their honor, insist on stripping to be searched thoroughly. One young and melancholy officer, Sasha, refuses to be searched although he vehemently asserts his innocence. He forces the others away from him at gunpoint, then leaves and shoots himself. The money is not found. Sasha had been wearing a portrait of his childhood sweetheart, who had recently married the colonel of the regiment, and he insisted on defending her honor by refusing to reveal his secret love. Only later do we learn that the money was stolen by a hotel servant.

The first half of the story is a well-knit and suspenseful mystery whose point of view allows suspicion to fall quite naturally first on Sasha and then on Avgust Matveich. Leskov makes a number of neat jibes at Russian prejudice toward the "untrustworthy" Poles, and indeed it is not until the end of the story that Avgust Matveich is cleared of suspicion and emerges as the man whose sense of honor is most genuine. But in the latter part of the story, beginning with chapter 9, the tone abruptly changes: the narrator reveals Sasha's secret and grows extraordinarily chatty, indulging in a series of pointless digressions which dissipate the tension. The story is a worthy one, but could have been much finer had Leskov exercised greater discipline and restraint in structuring it.

One of the most curious works in the cycle is "Po povodu 'Kreitserovoi sonaty'" (*À Propos* of The Kreutzer Sonata'), written, according to Andrey Leskov,[4] in 1890 under the title "The Lady from Dostoevsky's Funeral," but published only posthumously in 1899. The link with Tolstoy's tale of marital relations is established in the epigraph, a quotation from an early version of "The Kreutzer Sonata" which Leskov had read before its publication in 1891. The epigraph affirms the moral superiority of woman, a proposition which Leskov's story illustrates.[5] It is cast in the form of a personal memoir, although its factuality is dubious (some of the "autobiographical" data he provides contradict his actual biography). He describes a woman who came to him in a highly agitated state on the day of Dostoevsky's funeral. She had previously sought advice from the late writer and found solace in his work, but now turns to Leskov. She confesses that for the past eight years she has been unfaithful to her husband, and has suffered dreadfully from guilt. Leskov advises her to break off her affair but not destroy her family life by telling her husband. Several years later he encounters her, with husband and child, at a European resort. Here her son dies unexpectedly of diphtheria and she, totally distraught, kills herself.

The story is not without interest in itself, but even more so for what it reveals about Leskov's talents as a writer. It is essentially a psychological drama, but we are told so little about the woman's inner life and about her relationship to her husband (who appears to be a cold and unsympathetic character) that the drama falls flat. Leskov's gifts as an observer and storyteller did not equip him for the subtle and penetrating psychological analysis the situation demanded. An expert on guilt such as Dostoevsky, or a master of the nuances of male-female relationships such as Tolstoy, could have created a powerful story out of such material, but Leskov gives us only the surface of the events, and little enough of that. The story has an unfinished air, and Andrey Leskov suggests that Leskov may have intended to continue it by portraying the marriage from the husband's point of view. The ending — the widowed husband seems anxious to tell Leskov about his family — bears this out.

"Antuka" (1888) was originally conceived as a Tolstoyan story on pacifism. Leskov asked Tolstoy to help him locate material on a group of third-century pacifist Christians. He planned to write about a Russian sectarian who was inspired by his readings about these early Christians. When drafted into the army he chose martyrdom rather than act as executioner to a Pole and a Jew (11.390-92). Tolstoy never responded to Leskov's request, but the idea of the pacifist in military service was used in "Figura," while the motif of the executioner appears in a quite different light in "Antuka."

The story's epigraph explains its curious title: "*en tout cas*: an umbrella for any weather"; and it is told *à propos* of a discussion about the regrettable capacity of modern man to adapt himself to any circumstances. The principal narrator is Pan Honorat, who in his youth served with a band of Polish partisans led by a Catholic priest, Father Florian. Honorat is chosen by lot to execute two deserters and does so with little hesitation since he has no desire to become a martyr. He claims to suffer a few pangs of conscience afterwards, but now works as an Austrian gendarme, apparently willing to hang anyone for any reason. Here again, Leskov's desire to entertain comes into conflict with his urge to write a pacifist tract, and the former prevails. Honorat and Fr. Florian (a marvelous portrait of a thorough but ingenious scoundrel) are cast as the chief villains, totally cynical and prepared to change convictions when it proves advantageous. But the story is told with such verve and good humor that it is impossible to summon up much righteous indignation toward them. Much of the effect of the story — impossible to reproduce in summary — derives from its elaborate frame within a frame and the complex set of relationships between the narrator and his audience.

It is perhaps unfair to judge the stories *"à propos"* by the same standards as the rest of Leskov's fiction. In these, more than in any others, the boundary between fiction and journalism is blurred (indeed, a number of other works included in the cycle do not qualify as fiction at all). They were, for the most part, written in haste and designed to satisfy the growing appetite of middle-brow periodicals. The severe censorship of the 1880's also prevented Leskov from making his stories more explicitly *à propos* of contemporary events. The technique of beginning with a fragment of memoir material, a historical document or anecdote, and adding "the appropriate and necessary spices" (11. 430) is typically Leskovian. Such highly seasoned fare may not be to everyone's taste, and, to be sure, Leskov often uses a heavy hand when stirring in the spices. But they were a welcome relief from the frequently bland fare of the literary scene in the 1880's. The increasingly satirical tendency in these stories points the way to the final stage of Leskov's work.

Apart from the *à propos* cycle, Leskov published a number of other stories in the 1880's which were linked to specific events. "Tupeinyi khudozhnik" (The Toupee Artist, 1883), one of his most powerful and tragic stories, appeared on the anniversary of the decree emancipating the serfs, to which event it is dedicated. It is set in the early part of the century on the estate of Count Kamensky, renowned both for his elaborate serf theater and for his unbridled cruelty.It is told as Leskov's childhood recollection of a story told by his brother's nurse, Lyubov Onisimovna. In her youth Lyubov was an actress in Kamensky's theater and was in love with the "toupee artist" Arkady, the theater's talented hairdresser and makeup man. When it becomes clear that the count plans to include Lyubov in his harem, she and Arkady flee but are betrayed by a cowardly priest. Arkady is tortured and then sent off to the army; Lyubov is banished to the cattle sheds to tend the calves. Several years later Arkady returns as a decorated officer intending to buy her freedom, but before he can approach the count he is robbed and murdered by the keeper of the inn where he is staying.

Much of the story's power derives from its narrative technique: it is told in a simple and straightforward manner largely in the words of Lyubov herself while she sits on the grave of her lover. The narrator provides summaries and fills in factual information, but does not sentimentalize or over-dramatize the situation. The result is an economy of means, a directness and understatement rare in Leskov's writings. The only slightly false note is Arkady's murder, which comes as a total accident from outside the story and is included simply to heighten the tragedy. But the image of the old nurse sitting on the grave of her lover, sucking at the bottle that helps ease her grief, provides as grim a picture of the horrors of serfdom as one could wish for.

Leskov also wrote *à propos* of the famine and cholera epidemic of 1891-92. "Yudo," (The Vale of Tears, 1892) is an "autobiographical" series of anecdotes and incidents from an earlier and even more dreadful famine in 1840. It is subtitled "Rhapsody" — an apt description of its irregular composition and intense color. Leskov relates many incidents to demonstrate the ignorance and superstition which render the peasants helpless to combat the famine. The peasants are convinced that burning a candle of human fat will bring rain to save the dying crops, and murder a villager to obtain the ingredients. The authorities and landowners are equally helpless and indifferent to the plight of the starving: one landowner washes his seed grain with liquid manure so his peasants will not be able to eat it. Leskov emphasizes throughout the same point that Tolstoy makes in his writings on the famine — the real evil is "the hunger of the mind, the heart, and the spirit" (9. 297).

The only bright spot in this bleak scene is provided by Leskov's fictionalized "Aunt Polly" and her friend, the English Quakeress Hildegard, two of Leskov's most appealing positive characters. Aunt Polly has had a checkered past, but her readings of the Bible have convinced her that the real meaning of Christianity lies in active love and practical assistance to those in need. She and Hildegard seem the only ones capable of easing both the physical and the spiritual hunger of the people and Leskov describes their energetic measures with genuine respect. Even though much of the work consists of anecdotes about starvation, murder, and cannibalism, the overall effect is not one of total horror. Leskov's narrative talents enable him to tell this grisly tale with great verve and power and sometimes macabre humor. He closes with the hope that Polly's example will help assuage the spiritual hunger which will persist long after the famine has ended.

One other powerful story about the ignorance of the peasantry, "Produkt prirody" (A Product of Nature) was included in an 1893 collection of works by contemporary writers published to aid needy peasants being resettled in new areas. Leskov recounts an episode from his service with his uncle Scott when he accompanied a party of peasants who were being forcibly settled in the steppe lands. The peasants were transported by barge in crowded, filthy conditions, and were soon so badly tormented by lice that they were at the point of rebellion. The young Leskov sympathized with them and allowed a large group to go ashore to find a bathhouse. As soon as they moved out of sight, the whole group immediately set off back to their native villages. A clerk in the town manages to capture them without difficulty because, as he tells Leskov, he knows the people thoroughly:

I put on my overcoat with the big buckle, caught up with the fugitives and commanded them: "Get back, you swine!," brought them back and flogged the whole lot. My belt buckle has a marvelous effect. I drove them back like the Pharaoh of Egypt, brought them here and thrashed them. And don't forget that I thrashed them with their own magnanimous and gracious assistance. They held each other's legs and sat on one another's heads. Then I sent them back to the barges and it's all over. They sail off, and I stand on the shore and think "Oh you filthy Slavs! You worthless Russians!" Just let someone with a few helpers try a trick like that with forty Frenchmen. . . . And it's done, don't forget, just because of a simple buckle. But if I had had a real medal! Oh, if I had had a real medal! With a real medal I could flog the whole of Russia single-handed! (9.354)

The peasants are portrayed as a "product of nature" — an amorphous mass of raw humanity. Yet this totally unsentimental view does not prevent Leskov from arousing sympathy for the inhuman conditions in which the peasants were transported in the 1860's and in the 1890's. The biting satire on their passivity and total deference to any sort of authority, as well as on the petty "Pharaohs" who exploit this passivity, is one of the major themes of Leskov's satires of his last years.

III *Satires*

Leskov's concern with the didactic function of literature had led him to create whole series of moralistic works, and his encounter with Tolstoy's ideas only strengthened this tendency. But his "Tolstoyan" stories — *Prolog* tales, folktales, and tales of "righteous men" — are uneven and generally not his best work. Tolstoy's manner in literature was simply not Leskov's. Thus in the closing years of his life he again assessed his role as a writer, and in 1894 he wrote rather apologetically to Tolstoy that his talents were not those of an "interpreter of the Talmud." He had, however, resolved

to continue to do what I am capable of doing, that is "to help clean out the temple by driving out those who are trading in it." Kaulbach [Wilhelm von Kaulbach (1805-1874), German painter and illustrator] said this about himself, and it has long seemed to me appropriate to my intellect, spirit, and capacities. I cannot "reveal the one who dwells in the *sanctum sanctorum*" and believe that I should not undertake to do so... As I work on what I am now engaged in, that is, scraping away the droppings and the dirt from the "buyers and sellers" in the temple of the living God, I think that I am fulfilling a small part of my vocation, that is, a vocation in accordance with my resources, a vocation which I have already grown accustomed to manage with and in which I have achieved some success.[6]

The broom he used to sweep the temple took shape in a series of sharp satires published in the 1890's. Satire had, of course, been present in Leskov's writings from the very beginning, but his desire to "flog and torment" his contemporaries through his writings grew stronger and more pointed as he regarded with anger and disgust the life unfolding around him. He wrote to his confidant Sergey Shubinsky in 1883:

You write that I should not lose heart but must keep my spirits up. Of course that is true, but one cannot help but become weary. So many years of work and despondency have surely cost the body and soul something. I loved my native land, after all, and wanted to see it closer to goodness, to enlightenment and justice, but instead of that we see either disgusting indulgence in nihilism or shabby retreat "homewards," that is, to pre-Petrine stupidity and injustice. How can that "keep your spirits up?" There is but one solution: to despise and hate this native land and to be a philosopher and a cold-blooded man. But that cannot be achieved without torment. And there is not a ray of light in the sky; everywhere there is a minimum of ideas. All that is honest and noble has declined; it is harmful and is pushed aside. People who are only worthy of scorn are on the rise... Poor native land! With what sort of people will she meet her ordeals if they are fated for her? (11. 284-85)

The anger and bitterness of this letter do carry over into his fiction, although this may not be immediately obvious. Leskov's most common satirical technique was what he called a "slyly genial manner of narration" (11. 372) which masked his real intentions so well that some of his contemporaries complained "that in my stories, apparently, it is really difficult to distinguish good from evil and that at times it seems one cannot at all make out who is harming the cause and who is aiding it."[7] Some of his most vicious characters are portrayed as veritable angels, while he is a master at sustaining a cheerful narrative of how a good person is ruined by scoundrels. Likewise, the ironically happy ending in which all prosper through their villainy is one of the hallmarks of Leskov's satire. The reader must often be prepared, as William Edgerton remarks, "to reverse all the plusses and minuses in [the narrator's] system of values"[8] in order to perceive Leskov's point.

The earliest satire of note is *Smekh i gore* (Laughter and Woe, 1871), a long autobiography of Orest Vatazhkov, a good-natured and mild-mannered man who sees his life in Russia as a long series of surprises, or more aptly, as cruel practical jokes. The loosely structured form (Leskov calls it a "potpourri") owes a good deal to Gogol's *Dead Souls*, and enables Vatazhkov, in describing his travels through Russia, to cover almost the whole social spectrum both before and after the reforms of the 1860s. Thus he tells of his encounters with schools and universities, the central and the provincial bureaucracies, the tsar's secret police, the army, as well as of his meetings with peasants, journalists, writers, clergymen, and other members of the intelligentsia, both liberal and conservative. Vatazhkov is something of a foreigner, having spent his early life in Italy, and the "surprises" begin as soon as his mother brings him back to Russia at the age of nine. After schooling, where his memories are mostly of frequent beatings, he enters university and is denounced to the police by a friend, expelled, reinstated, and again expelled and forced to serve in the army until he manages to retire by having himself certified as mentally unstable. This section of the book is dominated by a marvelous creation, Postelnikov, the "sky-blue cupid," a Manilov-like character who asks of Vatazhkov "five million pardons" as he cheerfully admits that he has given his friend a forbidden book and then denounced him to save his own career in the secret police.

Vatazhkov flees abroad to recuperate but, his curiosity aroused by the exciting news of the reform era, returns to find new surprises. The Russia he saw under Nicholas I was a society ruled by brute force; Alexander's reforms have not dispensed with this guiding principle, but have so upset the social structure as to allow more people wider scope for intrigue and self-seeking. This latter half essentially revolves around the major question of the 1860s, the fate of the peasants. Vatazhkov is asked to prepare a project for improving medical services in the area where his estate is located. In so doing he encounters a cross section of opinion as he interviews various people: Vasiliev, a police officer who escapes from the unpleasantness around him into mystical religion (and ends in a mental hospital); Ostrozhdensky, a skeptical materialist doctor who says that the peasants' problems are "cold, hunger, and stupidity" and that they must first be cured of their stupidity by beatings; the Justice of the Peace, Gotovtsev, who proposes that hospitals be built in the same manner as he builds schools — by extracting them from the peasants as bribes; the Provincial Governor who wants only peace and quiet, and his nihilist-sympathizing wife ("All religions are nonsense; oxygen is the creator of all"); and General Perlov, a fire-breathing chauvinist who would flog the whole of Europe but who spends his days in petty feuding. Vatazhkov tries to pick his way through this ideological minefield but manages to trigger an explosion at every step. He is finally rewarded for his public spirit by being exiled from the province. His last surprise comes in Odessa, where he is beaten by chance on the street during a pogrom and dies.

The whole work is related with great exuberance and good humor, even when the subject is the blackest of villainy. Yet a chill undercurrent runs beneath this sparkling surface. Vatazhkov, a-nother innocent brought to ruin, seldom comments on the treachery, cruelty and stupidity he encounters at every step. He is good-

hearted, rather naive, and enough of foreigner to be continually
surprised at the reality of Russia. The reader is thus left to draw his
own conclusions. In spite of its many highly topical allusions and
the multiplicity of its targets, *Laughter and Woe* is a keen and
readable work of satire.

Leskov's next satirical work cost him no small amount of grief;
indeed, he was convinced that the censorship problems he experienced with it had shortened his life. In 1878 he published a series of
feuilletons later collected as *Melochi arkhiereiskoi zhizni* (Little
Things from Bishops' Lives). He notes that the formalized biog-
raphies written by church historians stressed only the piety and asceticism of bishops, but failed to make their subjects come alive.
He proposes to "defend" the higher orders of the clergy by revealing some of the "little things" of their lives, the human touches "in
which a man most reveals himself as a living person" (6. 535). Thus
he provides a series of anecdotes and "pictures from nature"
framed by commentaries pointing out the admirable qualities of his
subjects. The anecdotes, however, are most often designed to prove
quite the opposite. This device works well when it is used with some
subtlety, but too often it becomes only heavy sarcasm.

One of the finest is the third sketch describing the haughty
Bishop Varlaam, who was accustomed to terrify his subordinates
by his willful manner. Varlaam encounters Leskov's strong-willed
uncle Scott, and when Scott refuses to be cowed by the bishop's fit
of temper, Varlaam at once retreats and politely invites Scott for
tea. This proves beyond a doubt, Leskov notes slyly, that Varlaam
had simply been irritated by the obsequiousness of those around
him and was pleased to meet for the first time a man of true spirit.
Thus the slavish attitude of those who kowtow to rank is as much a
target as is the pomposity of the bishops themselves. At times
Leskov's efforts to reduce the bishops to human stature lead him to
scatological humor. Bishop Porfiry's elevated rank, for example,
does not permit him to walk. Through lack of exercise he suffers
dreadfully from constipation and resorts to an obstetrician who
"delivers" him of his problem. In other sketches Leskov does
portray some unpretentious bishops in a more favorable light, but
even here their simplicity is so overstated that they appear childish.
The obesity and pomposity of the bishops and their lack of
response to the real needs of the laity reflect the state of the church
as a whole. Leskov's efforts to humanize his bishops are typical of
his efforts to rid the church of its empty Byzantinism.

Leskov continued his anticlerical satire in a second cycle of stories, "Zametki neizvestnogo" (Notes from an Unknown Hand, 1884). These are written in an archaic style and are presented as the work of an anonymous chronicler whose tattered manuscript Leskov purportedly purchased from an antiquarian book dealer.[9] Any hope that this device would disarm the censor soon faded as the cycle of stories was broken off when the journal in which it was published faced closure.

The stories are uneven — some having a good deal of bite, others toothless — but many are good examples of Leskov's sly manner of satire. As in *Little Things*, the narrator's conclusion is often jarringly at variance with the real point of the story. Just as the story appears about to make a very serious point, the narrator draws back to state a quite innocent "moral." Thus in "Foreign Customs May Be Applied only with Caution," a young priest who has been educated abroad decides to introduce the Catholic practice of going into the details and circumstances under which a sin was committed while hearing the confessions of his parishioners. Another less sophisticated priest decides that he should follow the same practice. When a cook confesses that she once stole a timepiece from her employers and then swallowed it to prevent them from finding it in her room, he inquires: "Was it a wall clock or a pocket watch?" "Oh, Father," she replies, "where have you ever seen such a mouth that could swallow a wall clock! It might have started chiming down in my belly and then what would have become of me?" The priest agrees and decides that foreign practices are perhaps not so suitable for the Russians after all.

Although there are some very definite jibes at specific abuses in the church — its fear of innovation and Western influences, the whole "caste" system of inherited parishes, its power over citizens, particularly in matters such as marriage — most of Leskov's satire is directed against the manners of the clergy themselves. He delights in ridiculing them and portraying them as greedy, drunken, lazy, arrogant, and ignorant. The figure of Father Pavel, a cynical, malicious, and highly ingenious scoundrel, appears in several of the stories and sums up much of the worst of the clergy.

The same disarmingly innocent manner of narration occurs in "Ukha bez ryby" (Fish Soup Without Fish), originally published as a story "*à propos*" in 1886. The story might appear to be an anti-Semitic anecdote, but in fact the Jews and the Christians rival one another as scoundrels. Parasha, a young Ukrainian girl, lacks a

ruble to pay for the baptism of her illegitimate child. In such cases
the accepted custom was to stand on the town's bridge begging
from passersby: "The zealous do not refuse and each give a kopek.
If a hundred compassionate souls pass by, and if each gives a
kopek, then you have a hundred kopeks. And since the world is not
without good people after all, a girl is sometimes fortunate enough
to stand on the bridge with her unchristened child no more than
three or four days and by the fifth she has already scraped together
enough to buy a little baptismal cross and pay the baptizer."[10] But
Parasha has several competitors, and after eight days of standing in
the cold she appeals in despair to Solomon, the town's richest and
reputedly wisest Jew. Solomon's companion is amazed to see him
hand her a five-ruble note, asking her to bring the change. "How
could you!" exclaims his friend. "You, a firm and faithful Jew,
gave money to perform this offensive rite over a child?"[11] Solomon
explains it all: the five-ruble note was counterfeit. Thus everyone is
happy: Solomon has passed off the false note (which, he remarks,
was passed to him in a card game with the town's leading, Christian
citizens); the Jews are happy because they have such a wise man
among them; the Christians are pleased at Solomon's generosity;
and Parasha has her child baptized. The result is like fish soup
without fish: everyone gets a portion of the good, but somehow
something is missing.

A predominantly satirical mood dominates Leskov's final unfinished novel, *Chertovy kukli* (The Devil's Dolls). The work was
conceived as early as 1871, after he had completed *Laughter and
Woe*. Several early variants exist whose content differs considerably from that of the published version of 1890, but the basic idea
remained constant: Leskov wanted to treat a group of characters
whose lack of moral convictions deprives them of the will to resist
evil, something in the fashion of the German romantics (Leskov
mentions E.T.A. Hoffmann's *Serapion Brothers* as a model for the
work) who created dehumanized automatons who surrendered
their wills to some evil magician.[12] In later stages of the work
Leskov applied this idea to the relationship between the Russian
painter Karl Bryullov and Nicholas I and the work assumed its
present shape.[13] But by the late 1880s when the final touches were
being added to the novel, Leskov had had sufficient clashes with
the censor and so took pains to mask his references to real places
and people: the setting is an anonymous Duchy, the characters are
identified by non-Russian surnames (the central figure is Febufis,

that is, "son of Phoebus-Apollo"; his friends are Pik and Mak, etc.). But as he said, "knowledgeable people will understand what sort of a story this is. Its main element is depravity in the *seraglio* and the manners of a grandee of the *seraglio*. 'A struggle not with flesh and blood,' but simply depravity of the will accompanied by emptiness of the heart and outward dissimulation" (11.431).

Febufis is an artist whose reputation in Rome rests not only on his undoubted talent but also on his unrestrained character and daring escapades which have scandalized the city. A foreign duke traveling through Rome finds both Febufis's art and his manner appealing and invites him to live and work in his Duchy. What ensues is an animated account of how Febufis is inexorably drawn into the morass of life in the Duchy. The sinister power of the duke over all aspects of the lives of his subjects (masked by a solicitous concern for their welfare) is chillingly prophetic of later totalitarian regimes. Febufis is heaped with honors and privileges but finds his personal freedom ever more limited as the duke and his minions interfere even in the intimate details of his private life. The story breaks off before Leskov can tell us much about the promised "depravity in the seraglio," although it is clear that Febufis's fate is sealed once the iron doors of the Duchy have closed behind him.

What is clearly stated is the novel's second, allied theme, the role of art and the responsibility of the artist. Two other minor artists and friends of Febufis, Pik and Mak, are introduced early in the book to illustrate opposing views on the question. Although they are highly schematic characters, their views are of interest: "Mak was a thinker — he was concerned with social problems and grieved over the misfortunes of humanity and pondered over the social purposes of art. Pik, on the other hand, looked at life through rose-colored glasses and rejected all extraneous purposes in art aside from beauty itself" (8. 488). Pik also moves to the Duchy and suffers the fate of Febufis; Mak spurns fame, preferring to work quietly and maintain his dignity and independence. He is pleased enough that his small paintings hang only in taverns: "My genre-paintings keep me fed and they stir the odd person's conscience" (8. 529). The fate of Febufis illustrates this theme even more graphically. Just as the duke's patronage has restricted his personal freedom, so it limits the artistic freedom he once cherished. Stung by foreign criticism of his latest paintings, Febufis writes a stirring rebuttal defending "free art." The duke finds this superb but will not allow it to be published because, he explains, the tasks of art are to show heroism, pastorale, faith, the family, and the peacefully bucolic, and not stick its nose into social problems. This is your province, where you are kings and can do as you please. Historical paintings are also possible — I don't deny the historical as long as it is from our, true point of view, and not theirs. Art does not touch on social problems. The artist ought to stand above all that. Those are the sort of people we need! Seek out people who can be useful for art in such a fashion and summon them here. Providing for them is my concern. We could even give them ranks and uniforms. Here they can create unhindered, because there are no anxieties here, no disquiet. I want our school to preserve the genuine, pure artistic tradition and to set the tone for all others. To renew art — that is our vocation. (8. 538)

Leskov's account of the dilemma of the artist in a totalitarian society is remarkably modern.

Leskov took great pains in writing the novel and remained dissatisfied with its later parts, delaying publication for more than a year and finally abandoning it altogether.[14] The later parts were more specific in their references to Russia, and he was no doubt aware of the storm they would raise. Given the precarious state of his health and his need for total calm, he probably decided not to risk another crisis.

Risk of censorship also delayed the publishing of "Adminstrativnaia gratsiia" (Administrative Grace) until 1934. The story, based on the kind of scandalous anecdote from the past which Leskov loved, concerns the neat and quite vicious manner in which the governor of a town rids himself of a university professor whose liberal ideas and popularity are a potential source of trouble. The professor's archenemy is summoned to the office of a police colonel; the colonel is called out of the office on a matter of "urgent business," but leaves a letter on his desk alleging that the liberal professor is in the pay of the police. Before long the professor is hissed out of his lecture hall and soon commits suicide. The police colonel explains that there are two methods of subduing wild animals in the circus: *wilde Dressur*, in which the beasts are frightened with pistol shots and hot irons, and *zahme Dressur*, "in which not only are no shots fired but even the whip is cracked only for show. Yet the results are quite splendid..." (9. 393).

The narrative technique — the totally cynical ex-governor discusses the "happy ending" of the case with some pride — gives rise to much bitter irony. The ex-governor concludes: "For its part, the administration displayed genuine grace in this case. You see, if one

is graceful he can eat even the greasiest pie or sauce and not violate
the pristine whiteness of his tie or cuffs. Thus a measure of grace
will help the able administrator to settle the most unpleasant affair
in such a manner that not a single spot falls on his department, but
all of the spatters stay on the plate, that is, on the public itself" (9.
395-96). The satire lashes out in many directions: the plan is a
product of the local clergy who work in close cooperation with the
police; there are some acid comments about Leskov's former superiors in the government service, Dmitry Tolstoy and Ivan Delyanov.
But the real culprit in the vicious character assassination of the professor is the public itself, so fickle and easily led that its heroes can
become scapegoats overnight.

The fickle public is a very definite if scarcely visible ingredient of
"Polunoshchniki" (Nightowls, 1891). Indeed, the work as a whole
relies on an indirect method whose whole point lies in what is
unseen and unsaid. One of the characters around which it revolves,
a much sought after priest, is never mentioned by name (the characters refer only to "him"), although contemporaries would have
little difficulty in discerning the figure of Father Ioann of
Kronstadt. Father Ioann (Ivan Sergiev, 1829-1908) achieved an e-
normous reputation in the late nineteenth century for his reputedly
miraculous powers of healing and prophecy, and competition for
his advice was so keen that he was sometimes mobbed in the street.
Leskov believed that Father Ioann was a charlatan concerned only
to squeeze money from the crowds attracted to his vulgarized religion. Leskov's letters to Tolstoy in particular are full of venomous
remarks about this new popular idol. Father Ioann himself was
hostile to Tolstoy, and the latter is another unnamed figure whose
shadow falls over the work. For Leskov, of course, Tolstoy was all
that Father Ioann was not; the sincerity and simplicity of Tolstoy's
religious beliefs were the antipode to the shoddy mercantilism of
Father Ioann.

"Nightowls" is told largely in an indirect manner. We never see
the principals themselves but only eavesdrop on their late-night
conversations through the thin walls of an "*azhidatsiya*,"[15] a seedy
rooming house where suppliants await an audience with "him."
The detailed description of this institution, where icon-lamps and
geraniums fail to distract from the stale cooking odors, begins to
set the tone. The fragments of the first conversation firmly
establish it. We gradually piece together that the old couple next
door has come to "him" for advice on how to handle their

Tolstoyan son. But their main interest is profit; they have come with false credentials and plan to continue their fraud by selling what information they can squeeze out of the guests to the proprietress of the rooming house, who will presumably pass it on to "him" for even greater profit.

The bulk of the story is the conversation from the other room next door, and it also concerns petty scheming masked by piety. It is told by one Marya Martynovna with occasional interjections from her roommate, Aichka. Marya Martynovna's story is essentially quite simple: Klavdinka, a young woman of intelligence and spirit, has shocked her wealthy merchant family by turning her back on their way of life to become a Tolstoyan. Her family enlists the aid of "him" to bring her back to "true Christianity," but when she confronts "him" she emerges clearly the winner. That interest in this brief story spun out over so many pages never flags is due to Leskov's impressive narrative skills. Marya Martynovna, who was once a hanger-on in Klavdinka's family and is still a full-time busybody, is one of Leskov's great talkers, rivaled only by "The Amazon." In her telling, the story moves through a wealth of anecdotes, dizzying digressions, secondary characters, and hilarious fragments from her own checkered past. Her language, with its gush of mangled foreign terms and unintentional puns, makes one forget the dreary surroundings and the sordid nature of the tale she relates. If anything, the technique works so well that we forget Leskov's quite serious point and, dazzled by Marya Martynovna's verbosity, forget her vicious and totally unscrupulous nature (the ending shows that she does not shrink even from the idea of murder). The brilliant linguistic play not only gives the story its sparkle but is a major satirical device. Marya Martynovna's pretensions to gentility lead her to embellish her language, but the result as counterfeit as the pious atmosphere of the *azhidatsiya* itself.

The positive ideal in the story is also presented indirectly. Klavdinka's aversion to the vulgarity of her surroundings and her desire to work for something better is filtered through the mind of Marya Martynovna, who cannot comprehend why the girl should turn her back on the comfortable and complacent life of her family. Although her values are totally alien to Marya Martynovna, it is clear that Klavdinka is the only honest character in the story.

"Nightowls" is often regarded as a satire directed against Father Ioann, but Leskov's real target is something much larger, which also is not immediately visible in the story. It is the mentality of the mob, the "mouse-like scurrying of life" of the epigraph. Marya Martynovna is an ideal representative of that "smug, self-satisfied herd" Leskov spoke of and which he saw as ever eager to turn its back on the truth in the stampede toward a false prophet. Leskov's concern is ultimately with the same poverty of the spirit he wrote of in his stories of the famine of 1892.

Marya Martynovna at least brought vitality to her narrative, but "Zimniy den'" (A Winter's Day, 1894) is Leskov's darkest satire, with an atmosphere as bleak and cheerless as the brief Northern day on which it is set.[16] As Leskov said, the story "gives one neither rest nor peace" (11. 599). The editor of the journal to which he first offered it was dismayed by its near total concentration on various forms of depravity and declined to publish what he called "this excerpt from Sodom and Gomorrah."[17] Leskov once more deals with poverty of the spirit, but this time in a much more obvious and pernicious form involving not middle-class merchants but the topmost levels of society.

The structure of the work bears at least some similarity to that of "Nightowls," being a series of conversations between family members, visitors, and servants in the household of an aging society woman whose fortunes have ebbed. Characters come and go across the stage of the lady's St. Petersburg apartment, while the narrator remains "objective" in that he simply sketches in the scenes and provides information about externals. Much is left unsaid and some remains unclear, but this is an effective device since it suggests that the family has even darker secrets than those already revealed. In place of a developed plot we have a gradual revelation of the basic situation on which the work is built. Luka, the wealthy brother of the anonymous hostess, disapproves of his nephews (her sons) and plans to leave his money to Lidia, the lady's niece. What also emerges is a complex and sordid tangle of sexual and monetary relationships between the characters: the hostess's friend is blackmailing the hostess's Uncle Zakhar, her onetime lover, because of some compromising papers she holds; she, in turn, is being used by her young lover, the hostess's son Valery. (Her other son is a homosexual.) Valery has also seduced his mother's maid, who is preparing to sell herself to Uncle Zakhar. In the final scene the lady's cook indulges in her penchant for adolescent boys. It also appears that the guest is, or has been, a police spy, and she and the hostess are preparing to fabricate a case against Lidia to deprive her of Luka's legacy. This in fact provides the only plot in the work. Learning that Luka now plans to leave his money to charity (Lidia does not want it), mother and son begin to design a new plan to divert the money to themselves.

The single, small bright spot in this gloomy picture is the lady's niece, Lidia, an independent young woman who, apparently influenced by Tolstoy's teachings, is studying to be a medical assistant. Tolstoy's ideas once again form an implicit background and positive alternative to the moral decay which permeates all levels of society portrayed here. Tolstoy and Tolstoyans are subjects for gossip for the two ladies (not surprisingly, their spiritual guide is Father Ioann of Kronstadt), and the hostess's account of her former Tolstoyan maid is particularly revealing. Although the maid was an exemplary worker and accepted a very low wage, her insistence on telling the truth quickly began to undermine the lady's household, in which lies were so important. Lidia herself is critical of Tolstoy's followers who "just talk and talk and talk but never do anything worth a brass farthing" (9. 416).

Running through the story is the motif of the legacy, a motif with a spiritual as well as monetary dimension. Leskov shows how the younger generation inherits the moral rot from its elders and passes it, in turn, to the next generation. Thus the story's end in which the cook corrupts an adolescent shop boy. What emerges most strongly is the sense of a tired, decaying society bored by its own vices. Lidia declines to accept this legacy and looks elsewhere for support. Her sort of practical, selfless activity is the only salvation offered in the story.

Leskov once again manages to maintain interest in such a depressing picture through brilliant narrative technique. He captures precisely the tone of two aging and malicious society ladies, while the gradual revelation of the relationships between the characters keeps the reader's curiosity aroused. His technique owes something to Chekhov: the essentially dramatic structure relying mainly on dialogue with only brief "stage directions" from the narrator; the absence of a strongly developed plot; the sense that much more is going on behind the scenes than is disclosed; and the reliance on a series of recurring motifs (the exchange of money; the comments of the doorman; the kiss; Persia and the East as symbols of decadence) are all typical of Leskov's younger contemporary, but are relatively new in his own work. While Leskov never achieves Chekhov's subtlety and economy of means, this new direction in his art shows that he did not cease to grow even at the end of his literary career.

Another pessimistic view of the Russian mentality is expressed in "Zagon" (The Beast Pen, 1893). Leskov explains that his story is *à propos* of some current attempts to revive an old idea in Russian history: that Russia should "forget about the existence of other Western European states and separate herself from them by a Chinese wall" (9. 356). His title was inspired by a satirical drawing he once saw mocking an earlier but equally reactionary appeal for Russian isolationism. The drawing showed "a darkened cattle pen, surrounded by a wall with cracks in it here and there through which a few weak rays of light shone into the total darkness" (9. 357). The story itself concerns several of Leskov's own encounters with the obscurantist "beast-pen" mentality which deliberately closed itself off from enlightenment and progress in favor of moldering tradition and mindless superstition. The earliest of these occurred during his service with Scott and Wilkins when the Scotts were unable to persuade peasants to use a modern plow even after they demonstrated its superiority to the traditional wooden plow (*sokha*). A landowner builds neat brick cottages for his serfs who refuse to live in them, preferring to spend their last rubles to build chimneyless wooden huts in which they risk blindness and suffocation from smoke. Miller, a captured British officer who has survived the hazards of front-line fighting in the Crimea, meets his end walking down the sidewalk in Penza. Scott forgets to tell him why the local population prefers to wade through the knee-deep mud of the streets, so Miller is drowned when the sidewalk collapses and he falls into the sewer beneath. Some of Leskov's later experiences show that the mentality which preferred life in a smoky, vermin-infested hut to a clean brick building was by no means confined to the peasants. A group of well-bred generals' wives summering on the Baltic coast discover a new "prophet" in a wily, lazy, and thoroughly deceitful peasant, Mifimka, and bring their daughters to him for blessings and confession. The black humor of the work coexists with a very real pessimism, best summoned up by Scott:

Nothing that is good is of any use here because here lives a people that is barbarous and wicked.

   Not wicked, uncle!

   Yes, wicked. You are a Russian and perhaps you find this unpleasant, but I am a foreigner and I can judge dispassionately: this is a wicked people. But still, that is nothing: what is much worse is that they are told lies and convinced that what is bad is good and what is good is bad. Mark my words: there will be retribution for this, and when you least expect it! (9. 368-69)

Leskov's last work had an unusual narrative technique which, as in "Nightowls," masks a delicate subject. Indeed, "Zaiachii remiz" (The March Hare) was regarded by even liberal editors as so sensitive it was not published until 1917. It is told as the autobiography of a madman — or at least a resident of an asylum — Onopry Peregud, and the comic, Ukrainian-flavored language and farcical incident of his narrative masks a gloom as deep as that of "The Beast Pen." Peregud is the scion of an old Ukrainian Cossack family who, after an education by the "abridged" method in the bishop's choir, finds himself a district police officer. Peregud had never distinguished himself for intelligence, and his education has provided him with little more than an intricate knowledge of church ritual and an amazing recall of the number of saints' days celebrated each month. Nonetheless, he proves most adept at catching village horse thieves. Eventually he convinces himself that his village is being invaded by "shakers of the foundations and rockers of the thrones," and becomes obsessed with capturing such a nihilist for himself. He denounces a governess (whose seditious statements turn out to be Biblical quotations), two collectors of folk songs, and a secret policeman who is in the act of pursuing a real revolutionary, Peregud's own coachman. All this so unhinges him that he is sent to an asylum and spends the rest of his days knitting socks for the other inmates.

The satire is all the more effective because of its technique of reversal: the initial picture of Peregud, a peasant woman's kerchief on his head and his knitting on his knee, seems not so absurd after his account of the madness of the world around him. Peregud is heir to two unhappy legacies: the corrosive tradition of serfdom (a large part of his story is his comic account of how his great-grandfather made slaves of free Cossacks) and the dead weight of the church, whose representatives work hand in hand with temporal authority to shut out new ideas and keep people enslaved. "Good Lord, what man could stand it and remain sane?" remarks one of the more enlightened characters after hearing of Peregud's early life (9. 582). Even more important is the philosophical undercurrent in the story. The epigraph — from the Ukrainian religious philosopher Hrihory Skovoroda (1722-94) — concerns the difference between the ideal image of Man and the actual "coarse lump of clay" (*telesnyi bolvan*) in which that image manifests itself. Peregud's story reveals how the divine spark is extinguished by the "weight of the pyramids which the Pharaohs had piled up for themselves with the hands of slaves, tortured by hunger and the lash" (9. 591). Leskov points to the futility of pursuing external evil while ignoring the evil within. He is equally skeptical about Peregud's utopian dreams. Peregud speaks of his nocturnal flights to a swamp where he will hatch a firebird from a heron's egg (an old Russian folklore motif suggesting regeneration), but he admits that he has had no success: "There's too much pride in us, I'm afraid" (9. 588). As Skovoroda, the "Russian Socrates," insisted, one must first know oneself.

In spite of the story's unfinished air (the narrator refers to incidents which never occurred; characters reappear with altered names or titles; promised episodes are forgotten), and in spite of the obscurities caused by the thick camouflage he hoped would deceive the censor, "The March Hare" is an intriguing work because of its racy language, the range of its satire, and its philosophical depth.

Leskov's satires begin in the 1870's as spirited attacks on specific faults — largely on externals such as the manners of the clergy — and end as trenchant and bitter reflections on the flaws in human nature itself. The irony is that the liberal editors who ostracized the "reactionary" Leskov in the 1860's and 1870's feared to publish his "dangerous" writings in the 1880's and 1890's. Leskov's satires reflect his general stance as a writer who moved against the current of his times, mocking the follies of the liberals in a liberal era and ridiculing the absurdities of the conservatives in a conservative era. And he must be given due credit for his undoubted courage in affirming his unpopular views. But despite the changes in his targets, the underlying values of his satires remain the same: an ethic stemming from basic Christianity; the necessity for individual reform before meaningful social improvement can take place; the enlightened and free individual as the antithesis of the mindless mob.

CHAPTER 7

Conclusion

W HAT one remembers most about Leskov's writings is that
they are entertaining. His love of complex, seemingly unend-
ing tales whose plots expand by picking up ever more colorful incident, his fondness for stories within stories, fanciful flourishes, and
secondary incidents leading nowhere but included for the sheer
delight of telling them, give his work an almost Oriental flavor. As
a master storyteller he was concerned above all to capture and hold
the attention of his audience. "All types of literature are good," he
said, "except the boring types" (11. 352). Apart from curious
characters and engrossing incident, his stories rely on a whole range
of devices to sustain interest: intriguing titles and subtitles; unusual
epigraphs; openings which arouse curiosity; short chapters, often
ending at a crucial point to keep the reader reading.

But he conceived of literature as more than just superb entertain-
ment. As he remarked shortly before his death: "I love literature as
a means that allows me to express all that I consider to be true and
good. If I cannot do that then I no longer value literature.... I
absolutely cannot understand the principle 'art for art's sake.' No,
art ought to be of benefit; only then does it truly make sense."[1] The
benefit which his art was to bring was either to "flog and torment"
his readers into a great awareness of their moral failings, or to
inspire them to better things by creating positive examples of ethical behavior. The desire to teach his readers often conflicts with his
urge to entertain them, and the tension between the two damages
more than a few of his writings.

A concern for the relevance of his work to contemporary issues
also runs through his writings from the very beginning. "A literary
man," he said, "is in his way the secretary to his time..."[2] Almost
all of his work is *à propos* of something, so much so that it is often
difficult to determine where journalism ends and fiction begins.

Leskov demands not only relevance but also authenticity of his work; his stories must have the air of the real experience of real people. Thus his fondness for the memoir — his own or someone else's — to provide the raw canvas on which he can embroider at will and show "what really happened." As he said of "The Vale of Tears": "This is all true, but sewn together like the patchwork quilts the Orel market women sell behind St. Ilya's. The era is faithfully portrayed and thus the artistic aim has been achieved. . . . But it had to be called a 'memoir' in order to show that it was not a fabrication; it is a series of events from the same era and of the same nature collected into one tale."[3]

The quest for authenticity often led Leskov to create deliberately "unartistic" works, but that these were only achieved after painstaking labor and numerous revisions is not surprising. He tries to show that he is tipping the scales on the side of life rather than art, truth rather than poetry. Indeed, he appears almost to abhor the literary conventions of his day. He names his genres ("legend," "chronicle," "survey," "rhapsody," "novel-chronicle," "fairy tale," "potpourri," *"paysage et genre," "revue"*) to underline their unconventionality; his language clashed with the literary norms of the day; the settings of his works were far removed from those typical of current literature. All of these show Leskov's desire for originality, for uniqueness, and thus for authenticity.

Originality is one of the chief attributes of his characters as well. The cranks and eccentrics who populate his writings are attractive because they are unique. One token of their uniqueness may be some special talent, expressed with as much physical gusto as in breaking wild horses, with as much delicacy as in painting miniature icons, or as modestly as in inventing a good shoe polish. His righteous men are isolated figures, alienated from their fellows or choosing to live apart from them. They are "islanders" who have not been shaped by their environment and who exist as a challenge to the crowd. They stand, in fact, at the very opposite pole to the faceless mob of Leskov's peasant stories or to the "smug, self-satisfied herd" of his later satires. The characters he most admires are the independent ones who have sufficient courage of conviction to stand against the prevailing standards of their society as they follow the promptings of their conscience. They themselves do not seek to remold their society, only to do their duty to those nearest them, a duty conceived in basic Christian terms.

Although Leskov's characters often tell their own stories, they seldom reveal much about their inner selves. The characters themselves are often simple and spontaneous, little given to introspection, and the conflict in their lives is with the external world rather than an inner struggle. Even though religion is one of their major preoccupations, Leskov's heroes are not gnawed by doubt as are Dostoevsky's, nor engaged in earnest pursuit of truth, as are Tolstoy's. Leskov's approach to character is through externals, and inner workings are suggested through something concrete. Katerina Izmaylova's guilty conscience comes in the form of a fluffy cat; Savely Tuberozov's spiritual crisis is symbolized by a terrifying thunderstorm; Merkul Praottsev's vocation to pursue the ineffable leads him to crawl through the window after it; the bishop's spiritual rebirth in "At the World's Edge" comes when he is physically brought to life by his guide. Leskov approaches character visually (thus the many comparisons to paintings in his characterizations) and superficially, in the primary sense of the word. What his characters may lack in depth they make up for in the breadth and intensity of their experience. Given his preoccupation with the physical aspects of life, it is understandable that passion, eroticism (as much as was permissible within the prim conventions of the day), and physical violence bordering on sadism are prominent in his work.

But Leskov's characters reveal themselves most of all in their language. It is here that he truly excels. His ability to create a full-blooded character solely on the basis of speech (as, for example, in "Nightowls") is astounding. One's language, too, is a token of one's uniqueness. And Leskov's ear for the spoken language and his ability to re-create its nuances in print are unparalleled in Russian literature. He told his biographer: "People tell me that it is fun to read my works. That is because all of us — my characters and myself — have our own voices. The voice is 'pitched' in each of us correctly, or at least carefully. I am afraid to lose control when I write: thus my petty bourgeois speak in the manner of petty bourgeois and my lisping and burring aristocrats in their own fashion. And this is a gift in a writer. But exploiting it is not only a matter of talent but of tremendous labor. Man lives by words and we must know at which moments of psychological life which of us will use which words."[4] His instincts as a collector served him well as he gathered obsolete words, obscure technical terms, dialect words, bookish terms, slang, and professional jargon and lovingly fitted them into his narratives. His fascination with popular etymology and the corruptions of standard Russian under the impact of foreign terms unfamiliar to the untutored souls of Russia's obscure corners lends sparkle to many stories. Popular etymology appears as another form of folk art, as creative in its way as the legends which people make up about their local heroes.

Leskov's linguistic abilities were not much appreciated in his lifetime; contemporary critics found his prose not only strange but excessive. But his language has proven to be one of his truly lasting contributions to Russian literature and probably his greatest influence on later writers. Chekhov was one of his first students in this regard, and his early stories owe much to Leskov, as do the writings of another unjustly neglected writer, Alexei Remizov. Although Leskov did not invent the *skaz,* he was its most noted practitioner and provided models for Evgeny Zamyatin[5] and Mikhail Zoshchenko. His attitude to the word as something concrete whose full potential can be uncovered when it is held up, examined, and toyed with, gained respect among the linguistic experimenters of the first decades of the twentieth century, who acknowledged him as one of the pioneers of "ornamental prose."

Apart from his linguistic influence, Leskov changed Russian literature by introducing fresh material into it. Unlike his contemporaries, he did not specialize in one or two areas of life, but ranged far afield, collecting clergymen, merchants, civil servants, soldiers, Jews, Germans, Englishmen, aristocrats, peasants, contemporaries, men of Tsar Nicholas's era, people from early Christian times. As Boris Eykhenbaum wrote:

Without him our literature of the nineteenth century would have been incomplete, first and foremost because it would not have been able to capture in sufficient measure Russia's out-of-the-way places with their "enchanted pilgrims"; it would not have revealed with sufficient fullness the souls and fates of Russians with their daring, their scope, their passions, and their misfortunes. There would not have been what Leskov himself liked to call "genre" (by analogy with genre painting), and this "genre" would not have been created so colorfully, with such diversity, and, in its own way, so poetically. Neither Turgenev, nor Saltykov-Shchedrin, nor Tolstoy, nor Dostoevsky could have done this as Leskov did it, although in the writings of each of them this task is present as a very important one for the era: to portray not only Russia but also Rus.[6]

Notes and References

Chapter One

1. Nikolai Leskov, "Avtobiograficheskaia zametka," *Sobranie sochinenii,* 11 vols. (Moscow, 1956–58), XI, 12. Further references to this edition are included in the text using volume number and page.
2. Andrei Leskov, *Zhizn' Nikolaia Leskova* (Moscow, 1954), p. 31.
3. Gostomlia: a small river in southern Orel Province; more generally, Leskov often uses it to describe the area around the Panino estate.
4. Andrei Leskov, *Zhizn' Nikolaia Leskova,* p. 73.
5. Jozef Ignacy Kraszewski's peasant stories played some part in Leskov's early fiction; the chatty, orally structured manner of some of the writings of Syrokomla (Ludwik Kondratowicz) and Zygmunt Kaczkowski is reflected in the development of Leskov's *skaz;* Kaczkowski's loosely structured novels and the Polish tradition of "memoir" literature in general influenced Leskov's chronicles.
6. The name Olga is reserved for some of the least appealing women in Leskov's writings.
7. A researcher on Leskov's links with Kiev, L. Levandovskii, argues that Leskov's early muckraking journalism led to his dismissal from his post. See "N. S. Leskov v Kieve (Novye materialy)," *Russkaia literatura,* No. 3 (1963), 104–109.
8. "The 1860s" as a distinct historical period actually begin in 1855, with the accession to the throne of Alexander II and the sudden rise in expectations of thorough reforms, and end in April 1866, with the terrorist Dmitry Karakozov's attempt on Alexander's life, signaling a sharp move to the right in government policy.
9. N. V. Shelgunov, *Vospominaniia* (Moscow-Petrograd, 1923), p. 163.
10. "O prodazhe evangeliia na russkom iazyke po vozvyshennym tsenam," *Sankt-Peterburgskie vedomosti,* No. 135 (1860), pp. 699–700.
11. "Zametka o zdaniiakh," *Sovremennaia meditsina,* No. 29 (1860), 513–23.
12. Respectively, "Neskol'ko slov ob ishchushchikh kommercheskikh mest v Rossii," *Ukazatel' ekonomicheskii,* No. 50 (1860), 858–60; "O rabochem klasse," *Sovremennaia meditsina,* No. 32 (1860), 561–69; "Vopros ob iskorenenii p'ianstva," *Ukazatel' ekonomicheskii,* No. 220 (1861), 135; "Neskol'ko slov o mestakh rospivochnoi prodazhi khlebnogo

151

vina, vodok i meda," *Ukzatel' ekonomicheskii,* No. 203 (1860), 805–7.

13. "Neskol'ko slov o vrachakh rekrutskikh prisutstvii," *Sovremennaia meditsina,* No. 36 (1860), 633–45.

14. "Neskol'ko slov o politseiskikh vrachakh v Rossii," *Sovremennaia meditsina,* No. 39 (1860), 689–99. Angry rebuttals and countercharges enlivened the pages of the staid medical journal through the rest of the year.

15. "Vospominaniia o P. Iakushine," *Sochineniia Pavla Iakushina* (St. Petersburg, 1884), p. 50.

16. O zamechatel'nom, no neblagotvornom napravlenii nekotorykh sovremennykh pisatelei," *Russkaia rech',* No. 60 (1861), 126–28.

17. Research has yet to find a convincing explanation for the St. Petersburg fires, with theories ranging from arson by radicals, to arson by police *agents-provocateurs,* to arson by merchants hoping to collect insurance, to accident. Two valuable studies are: Solomon Reiser, "Peterburgskie pozhary 1862 goda," *Katorga i ssylka,* No. 19 (1932), 79–107, and N. G. Rozenblium, "Peterburgskie pozhary 1862 g. i Dostoevskii (Zapreshchennye tsenzuroi stat'i zhurnala 'Vremia')," *Literaturnoe nasledstvo, 86: F. M. Dostoevskii. Novye materialy i issledovaniia* (Moscow, 1973), pp. 16–54.

18. A. V. Nikitenko, *Zapiski i dnevnik* (St. Petersburg, 1893), II, 327.

19. *Severnaia pchela,* No. 143 (May 30, 1862). The stilted style of this article, so uncharacteristic of Leskov, suggests the emotion and the haste with which it was written.

20. Andrei Leskov, *Zhizn' Nikolaia Leskova,* p. 149.

21. "Iz odnogo dorozhnogo dnevnika," *Severnaia pchela,* Nos. 334, 335, 337, 338, 339, 343–51 (1862); No. 108 (1863). "Russkoe obshchestvo v Parizhe," *Biblioteka dlia chteniia,* 178, No. 5 (1863), 1–31, and No. 6, 1–38; 179, No. 9 (1863), 1–56.

22. "Pestrye zametki," *Biblioteka dlia chteniia,* 175, No. 1 (1863), 210.

23. *O raskol'nikakh goroda Rigi, preimushchestvenno v otnoshenii k shkolam* (St. Petersburg, 1863).

24. "Nikolai Gavrilovich Chernyshevskii v ego romane *Chto delat'?"* X, 13–22.

25. The epigraph, the proverb "The Devil is not so fearsome as he is painted," also bears out this interpretation. G. Tamarchenko, *"Chto delat'?* Chernyshevskogo i *Nekuda* Leskova," *Voprosy literatury,* No. 9 (1972), 93–110, makes some interesting comments in this regard.

26. *Shestidesiatye gody. Materialy po istorii literatury i obshchestvennomu dvizheniiu* (Moscow-Leningrad, 1940), p. 354.

27. V. Zaitsev, "Perly i adamanty russkoi zhurnalistiki," *Russkoe slovo,* No. 6 (1864), 48.

28. "Progulka po sadam rossiiskoi slovesnosti," *Russkoe slovo,* No. 3 (1865), 15–16.

29. Quoted in Andrei Leskov, *Zhizn' Nikolaia Leskova,* pp. 178–79.

30. Most of these articles are unsigned and have been attributed to Leskov only recently by I. V. Stoliarova. See "N. S. Leskov v *Birzhevykh vedomostiakh i verchernei gazete* (1869–1871 gg.)," *Uchenye zapiski Leningradskogo gos. universiteta,* No. 295, vyp. 58 (1960), pp. 87–119, and "N. S. Leskov v *Russkom mire* (1871–5)," *Uchenye zapiski Omskogo gos. ped. instituta,* 17 (Omsk, 1962), pp. 97–122.

31. Andrei Leskov, *Zhizn' Nikolaia Leskova,* p. 295.

32. *Ibid.,* p. 370.

33. "Iezuit Gagarin v dele Pushkina," *Istoricheskii vestnik,* No. 8 (1886), 269–73.

34. "Velikosvetskii raskol," *Pravoslavnoe obozrenie,* Nos. 9–10 (1876), 138–78, 300–326; No. 2 (1877), 294–334.

35. Andrei Leskov, "N. S. Leskov," *Literaturnyi sovremennik,* No. 3 (1937), p. 157.

36. A. I. Faresov, *Protiv techenii. N. S. Leskov, ego zhizh', sochineniia, polemika i vospominaniia o nem* (St. Petersburg, 1904), p. 382.

37. Andrei Leskov, *Zhizn' Nikolaia Leskova,* p. 436.

38. *Ibid.,* p. 590.

39. "Russkie obshchestvennye zametki," *Birzhevye vedomosti,* No. 340 (Dec. 14, 1869).

40. Chertkov was a former guards officer who became Tolstoy's disciple, his close confidant, and, in effect, his business manager for most of Tolstoy's later life. He also managed *The Intermediary,* a publishing business producing cheap editions of good reading matter for the masses.

41. *Tolstovskii ezhegodnik 1913 g.,* II (St. Petersburg, 1914), p. 53.

42. Quoted in Andrei Leskov, *Zhizn' Nikolaia Leskova,* p. 606.

43. L. Ia. Gurevich, "Lichnye vospominaniia N. S. Leskova (iz dnevnika zhurnalista)," *Severnyi vestnik,* No. 4 (1895), p. 68.

44. *Ibid.*

45. *Ibid.,* pp. 65–66.

46. Andrei Leskov, "N. S. Leskov," 160.

47. *Ibid.,* p. 157.

48. *Ibid.,* p. 158.

49. Letter to A. S. Suvorin, Apr. 12, 1888. *Pis'ma russkikh pisatelei k A. S. Suvorinu* (Leningrad, 1927), p. 66.

50. Andrei Leskov, *Zhizn' Nikolaia Leskova,* p. 671.

Chapter Two

1. Leskov was aware of the shortcomings of the story and partially reworked it but never republished it in his lifetime. His abbreviated second version was later published by P. V. Bykov as *Amur v lapotochkakh. Krest'ianskii roman. Novaia neizdannaia redaktsiia* (Leningrad, 1924).

2. Dostoevsky's St. Petersburg has also worked its way on Leskov.

3. *Skaz:* Hugh McLean's definition, provided in "On the Style of a Leskovian Skaz," *Harvard Slavic Studies,* II (Cambridge, Mass. and The Hague, 1954), 297–322, is both succinct and well grounded: "a stylistically individualized inner narrative placed in the mouth of a fictional character and designed to produce the illusion of oral speech" (p. 299). Leskov's *skaz* is usually an "inner narrative" (the *skaz* is "framed" by a narrative in a neutral style), although this is not always the case with other writers. *Skaz* has been treated extensively by Soviet and Western scholars. Some worthwhile studies are: B. M. Eikhenbaum, "Illiuziia skaza," *Skvoz' literaturu: sbornik statei* (Leningrad, 1924), pp. 152–56; B. M. Eikhenbaum, "Leskov i sovremennaia proza," *Literatura. Teoriia. Kritika. Polemika* (Leningrad, 1927), pp. 210–25; V. V. Vinogradov, "Problema skaza v stilistike," *Poetika: sbornik statei* (Leningrad, 1926), pp. 24–40; Irvin R. Titunik, "The Problem of 'Skaz' in Russian Literature," Diss. Univ. of California, Berkeley, 1963; Martin P. Rice, "On 'skaz'," *Russian Literature Triquarterly,* 12 (Spring, 1975), pp. 409–24.

4. The word *doilets* is Leskov's creation. The feminine form, *doilitsa,* is an archaic term meaning "wet nurse." The root of the word refers to milking a cow.

5. Described in Leonid Grossman, *N. S. Leskov: Zhizn' — Tvorchestvo — Poetika* (Moscow, 1945), pp. 150–51.

Chapter Three

1. Leskov's fictionalized commune was closely modeled on the "Znamensky commune" established by the writer Vasily Sleptsov in 1863. Memoirs of participants reveal that Leskov's portrait was not unduly exaggerated. See Ekaterina Zhukovskaia, *Zapiski* (Leningrad, 1930); K. Chukovskii, "Istoriia Sleptsovskoi kommuny," *Liudi i knigi shestidesiatykh godov* (Leningrad, 1934).

2. For detailed discussion of the anti-nihilist novel see Charles A. Moser, *Antinihilism in the Russian Novel of the 1860's* (The Hague, 1964).

3. Artur Benni is also the subject of Leskov's *Zagadochnyi chelovek* (An Enigmatic Man, III, 276–381), a *biographie* more than a little *romancée* published in 1870. See Hugh McLean, "Leskov and his Enigmatic Man," *Russian Thought and Politics: Harvard Slavic Studies,* IV (Cambridge, Mass., 1957), 203–24, and Solomon Reiser, *Artur Benni* (Moscow, 1933).

4. Faresov, *Protiv techenii,* p. 66.

5. N. S. Leskov, *Polnoe sobranie sochinenii,* 36 vols. (St. Petersburg, 1902–1903), VI, 133–34. Hereafter this edition will be cited in the text as "PSS." The motifs Leskov lists here were common in novels of radicals of the day, most notably in Chernyshevsky's *What is to be Done?*

6. Leskov had mixed feelings about Dostoevsky the writer as did Dos-

toevsky about Leskov, a relationship one might expect between two writers who share so many concerns but whose methods are so different. There are several good studies of the topic: K. P. Bogaevskaia, "N. S. Leskov o Dostoevskom (1880-e gody)," *Literaturnoe nasledstvo, 86: F. M. Dostoevskii. Novye materialy i issledovaniia* (Moscow, 1973), pp. 606–20; E. M. Pul'khritudova, "Dostoevskii i Leskov (K istorii tvorcheskikh vzaimootnoshenii)," *Dostoevskii i russkie pisateli: Traditsii. Novatorstvo. Masterstvo. Sbornik statei* (Moscow, 1971), pp. 87–138; I. P. Viduetskaia, "Dostoevskii i Leskov," *Russkaia literatura,* No. 4 (1975), pp. 127–37; V. V. Vinogradov, "Dostoevskii i Leskov (70-e gody XIX veka)," *Russkaia literatura,* No. 1 (1961), pp. 63–84 and No. 2 (1961), pp. 65–94.

7. Compare Tolstoy's views expressed in an unpublished foreword to an early version of *War and Peace:* "The work offered here is closest in nature to a novel or tale, but it is not a novel because I simply cannot nor do I know how to set fixed limits on the characters I have invented — that is, either a marriage or a death, after which the interest in the narrative should cease. I could not help but realize that the death of one character only aroused interest in the others and that a marriage represented more of a beginning than an end" (*Polnoe sobranie sochinenii [Iubileinoe izdanie]*, XII [Moscow, 1949], p. 55.).

8. Quoted in Vinogradov, "Dostoevskii i Leskov," p. 75.

9. Bodo Zelinsky analyzes the plot in detail in this manner. See *Roman und Romanchronik: Strukturuntersuchungen zur Erzählkunst Nikolaj Leskovs* (Cologne and Vienna, 1970), pp. 183–232.

10. "*Cathedral Folk:* Apotheosis of Orthodoxy or its Doomsday Book," in Michael S. Flier, ed., *Slavic Forum: Essays in Linguistics and Literature* (The Hague, 1974), pp. 130–48.

11. Faresov, *Protiv techenii,* p. 340.

12. Leskov's dating, often unreliable, here too proves inaccurate. Pugachev was executed in 1775, eight years before the events described.

13. A third unfinished novel, *The Devil's Dolls,* is discussed in chapter 6. One more uncompleted novel and other previously unpublished writings appear in *Literaturnoe nasledstvo,* 87 (Moscow, 1977), 36–158.

14. *Gazeta A. Gattsuka,* 9, Nos. 7–10 (1883).

15. *Gazeta A. Gattsuka,* 9, No. 10 (1883), p. 206.

16. *Nov',* 1, Nos. 1–2 (November 1884).

17. I. Em, "Kak rabotaiut nashi pisateli: N. S. Leskov," *Novosti i birzhevaia gazeta,* No. 49 (Feb. 19, 1895), p. 2.

Chapter Four

1. "O khudozhnom muzhe Nikite i o sovospitannykh emu," *Novoe vremia,* No. 3389 (1886).

2. As Leonid Grossman points out (*N. S. Leskov,* pp. 170–71), "pri-

vate" persecution of Old Believers was not likely, nor would the officer who confiscated the icon have tried to extort money from the group before witnesses.

3. See "Smiatennyi vid," *Dnevnik pisatelia, Sobranie sochinenii,* XI (Moscow-Leningrad, 1929), 55–57.

4. For a fuller discussion of the story and its ending see Hugh McLean, "Russia, the Love-Hate Pendulum and 'The Sealed Angel,' " *To Honor Roman Jakobson* (The Hague, 1967), pp. 1328–39.

5. To use E. M. Forster's terminology, Flyagin relates his adventures as a "story"; it is up to his readers to discern that they in fact do form a "plot." A detailed study of the plot is M. P. Cherednikova, "O siuzhetnykh motivirovkakh v povesti N. S. Leskova 'Ocharovannyi strannik,' " *Russkaia literatura,* 3 (1971), pp. 113–27.

6. Thus "pilgrim" is a better translation here for the Russian *strannik* than "wanderer" since it implies one who travels with a very definite purpose.

7. An untranslatable pun on *kon'* ("horse") and connoisseur.

8. "Leskov," *Oxford Slavonic Papers,* 10 (1962), p. 20.

9. This work contains echoes of Dostoevsky's Christianity with its emphasis on mercy and voluntary assumption of the sufferings of another. To be sure, Flyagin's sufferings are more physical than spiritual, yet they ultimately lead to his salvation. The effect of his capricious will also has Dostoevskian overtones. The parallels seem more a result of an inherent affinity of outlook and reliance on a similar tradition in Orthodoxy than of conscious influence.

10. The degree to which the Leskov who narrates the story can be identified with the real Leskov cannot be definitely established, although his attitude toward the Jews was certainly equivocal. His background no doubt predisposed him to anti-Semitism, and his early journalism contains more than a few derogatory remarks about the Jews. In the 1880s, however, he published a series of newspaper articles explaining aspects of Judaism with much sympathy and understanding ("Religioznye obriady evreev," *Peterburgskaia gazeta,* Nos. 244, 245, 252, 254, 255 [1880]). Other articles on the Jews appeared here in 1881, 1884, and 1885). In 1883 a group of St. Petersburg Jews asked him to write a study of the Jewish situation in Russia for presentation to the "Palen Commission" examining laws pertaining to Jews. The study (*Evrei v Rossii: Neskol'ko zamechanii po evreiskomu voprosu* [St. Petersburg, 1884]) defended Jewish rights and called for an end to restrictions on settlement. He expressed his own contradictory attitude to Faresov: "I believe that it is best to live in brotherhood with all nationalities, and I express that opinion publicly. But I myself fear the Jews and avoid them. I am in favor of equal rights but I am not in favor of the Jews" (*Protiv techenii,* p. 300). Leskov's fictional treatment of Jews is examined in more detail by Hugh McLean, "Theodore the Christian looks at Abraham the Hebrew: Leskov and the

Jews," *California Slavic Studies,* VII (Berkeley, 1973), 65–98.

11. A term used to describe various evangelical and pietist sects which spread in the Ukraine and Southern Russia in the nineteenth century. Their example of charity, practical Christianity, and reliance on individual reading of the Gospels won over many who were disillusioned with Orthodoxy.

12. See, for example, Hugh McLean's interpretation of "The Enchanted Pilgrim" in these terms in "Leskov and the Russian Superman," *Midway* (Spring, 1968), pp. 105–23.

13. See E. S. Litvin, "Fol'klornye istochniki 'Skaz o kosom Levshe i o stal'noi blokhe' N. S. Leskova," *Russkii fol'klor: materialy i issledovaniia,* I (Moscow-Leningrad, 1956), 125–34; B. Bukhshtab, "Ob istochnikakh 'Levshi' N. S. Leskova," *Russkaia literatura,* No. 1 (1964), pp. 49–64; V. Shklovskii, "Ob odnoi tsekhovoi legende," *Ogonek,* No. 19 (1947), p. 16.

14. The most successful English translation is William Edgerton's in *Satirical Stories of Nikolai Leskov* (New York, 1969), pp. 25–53.

15. "Blagorazumnyi razboinik (Ikonopisnaia fantaziia)," *Khudozhestvennyi zhurnal,* 5, No. 3 (March 1883), p. 197.

Chapter Five

1. The saying probably originates in the Biblical account of Abraham's plea to God to spare Sodom if but ten righteous men can be found in the city (Gen. 18: 16–33).

2. "O geroiakh i pravednikakh," *Tserkovno-obshchestvennyi vestnik,* No. 129 (1881), p. 5. According to legend, in 362 B.C. Marcus Curtius threw himself into a crevice on Rome's forum to propitiate the gods and save the city.

3. Faresov, *Protiv techenii,* p. 381.

4. The subject is examined in more detail by Stephen S. Lottridge, "Nikolaj Leskov and the Russian *Prolog* as a Literary Source," *Russian Literature,* 3 (1972), pp. 16–39; and in his "Nikolaj Leskov's Moral Vision in the *Prolog* Tales," *Slavic and East European Journal,* 18 (Fall, 1974), 252–58.

5. Letter to V. G. Chertkov, June 20, 1887. (*Polnoe sobranie sochinenii (Iubileinoe izdanie),* LXXXVI (Moscow, 1937), 62–63.

6. *Ibid.,* XXXIV, 135.

7. *Ibid.,* LXV, 198.

Chapter Six

1. Not all the works originally written as Christmas stories were included here, for example, "The Sealed Angel" and "At the Edge of the

World." Two stories that were included, "The Bogey-Man" and "Figura," are discussed in chapter 5.

2. A more detailed reading of the story in this manner can be found in Katherine Tiernan O'Connor, "The Specter of Political Corruption: Leskov's 'White Eagle,' " *Russian Literature Triquarterly,* 8 (1974), pp. 393–406.

3. See, for example, his articles in *Istoricheskii vestnik* in the 1880s.

4. Andrei Leskov, *Zhizn' Nikolaia Leskova,* p. 371.

5. Leskov always placed great stress on a woman's capacity to inspire solid moral principles in her family. In an early piece of journalism he wrote: "We need good wives and mothers. Russia is in greater need of them than she is of brilliant generals and ministers. Our country is such that its strength lies in the family; our ways are such that we revere a woman most of all for her virtues as a mother and our genuine Russian will not renounce this ideal. . . . A happy family is the closest and most legitimate ideal of the Russian" ("Spetsialisty po zhenskoi chasti," *Literaturnaia biblioteka,* 12 [1867], p. 274).

6. S. P. Shesterikov, ed., *Pis'ma Tolstogo i k Tolstomu. Iubileinyi sbornik* (Moscow-Leningrad, 1928), p. 165.

7. "Ukha bez ryby," *Nov',* 8, No. 7 (February 1886), p. 352.

8. Edgerton, *Satirical Stories of Nikolai Leskov,* p. 239.

9. It seems, as William Edgerton suggests (*Ibid.,* p. 161), that the inspiration for the work did come from an eighteenth-century manuscript which Leskov purchased in 1883 (see XI, 288). The manuscript, "Istoriia semi mudretsov," was written in 1772 (not 1702, as Leskov says) and is described in *Opisanie rukopisnogo otdela BAN SSSR,* IV, vyp. 1 (Moscow-Leningrad, 1951), pp. 364–65. However, Leskov borrowed little more from it than the basic concept of a series of novellas told in an archaic style.

10. *Nov',* 7, No. 7 (1886), p. 355.

11. *Ibid.,* p. 357.

12. The most complete description of the early versions of the novel is in I. V. Stoliarova and A. A. Shelaeva, "K tvorcheskoi istorii romana N. S. Leskova 'Chertovy kukly,' " *Russkaia literatura,* No. 3 (1971), pp. 102–13. Also see K. P. Bogaevskaia's comments in *Literaturnoe nasledstvo,* 86 (Moscow, 1977), 36–40.

13. Comments on the relationship between fictional characters and their historical prototypes can be found in S. Eleonskii, "Nikolai I i Karl Briullov v 'Chertovykh Kuklakh' N. S. Leskova," *Pechat' i revoliutsiia,* No. 8 (1928), pp. 37–57.

14. Stoliarova and Shelaeva have described the remaining unpublished portions of the novel which have survived in manuscript. Court gossip links Geliya, Febufis's wife, with the Duke, and the artist becomes an object of ridicule. He manages to escape to Rome to avoid arrest but finds his artistic inspiration has abandoned him and ends by suicide. Pik and

Mak both become ardent supporters of Garibaldi and Febufis's illegitimate son dies as a soldier in Garibaldi's army. (See also Shelaeva's notes in N. S. Leskov, *Sobranie sochinenii v shesti tomakh,* V (Moscow, 1973), 414–19.)
15. Hugh McLean's translation, "expectension," is the nearest English approximation. (Edgerton, *Satirical Stories,* p. 243.)
16. Vsevolod Setschkareff makes some interesting comments about Schopenhauer's influence on Leskov in this story (*N. S. Leskov: Sein Leben und sein Werk* [Wiesbaden, 1959], p. 153).
17. Quoted in Andrei Leskov, *Zhizn' Nikolaia Leskova,* p. 563.

Chapter Seven

1. *Peterburgskaia gazeta,* No. 326 (Nov. 27, 1894), p. 3.
2. "Russkie obshchestvennye zametki," *Birzhevye vedomosti,* No. 242 (1869), p. 2.
3. Letter to V. L. Ivanov, Aug. 7, 1892. (Quoted in O. Bilets'kyi, "Rasskazy i ocherki N. S. Leskova," *Zibrannia prats' u p'iaty tomakh,* IV [Kiev, 1966], p. 385.)
4. Faresov, *Protiv techenii,* p. 274.
5. Zamyatin pays tribute to Leskov in *Blokha* (The Flea), his sparkling dramatization of "Lefty."
6. "N. S. Leskov (k 50-letiiu so dnia smerti)," *O proze; sbornik statei* (Leningrad, 1964), p. 348.

Selected Bibliography

PRIMARY SOURCES

1. In Russian

LESKOV, N. S. *Polnoe sobranie sochinenii.* 3d. ed. 36 vols. St. Petersburg: A. F. Marks, 1902–1903. The most complete edition of Leskov's fiction. Unannotated.

————. *Sobranie sochinenii v odinnadtsati tomakh.* Moscow, 1956–58. Major fiction, selected journalism, and letters. Detailed and useful (if occasionally erratic) notes.

2. In English

————. *The Amazon and Other Stories.* Transl. David Magarshack. London: George Allen & Unwin, 1949. Also contains "A Little Mistake" and "The March Hare."

————. *The Cathedral Folk.* Transl. Isabel Hapgood. (1924; rpt. Westport, Conn.: Greenwood Press, 1971). The only English translation of Leskov's best-known novel.

————. *The Enchanted Pilgrim and Other Stories.* Transl. David Magarshack. London and New York: Hutchinson, 1946. Also contains "A Will of Iron," "Deathless Golovan," "Lefty," and "The Toupée Artist."

————. *Satirical Stories of Nikolai Leskov.* Transl. and ed. William B. Edgerton. New York: Pegasus, 1969. Fine translations with valuable introduction and notes.

————. *Selected Tales.* Transl. David Magarshack. Intro. V. S. Pritchett. New York: Farrar, Straus and Cudahy, 1961. "Lady Macbeth," "The Enchanted Pilgrim," "Lefty," "The Sentry," "The White Eagle."

SECONDARY SOURCES

The items listed below are of a more general nature. For other studies of specific works, consult the notes.

ANSBERG, ALEKSEJ B. "Frame Story and First Person Story in N. S. Leskov." *Scando-Slavica,* 3 (1957), 49–73. Language and narrative technique; brief analyses of individual stories.

BENJAMIN, WALTER. "The Story-Teller: Reflections on the Works of Nicolai Leskov." *Chicago Review,* 16 (1963), 80–101. A stimulating essay on Leskov and the art of storytelling generally.

CAVAION, DANILO. *N. S. Leskov. Saggio critico. Publicazioni della Facolta di Magistero dell' Universita di Padova,* 21. Florence: G. C. Sansoni, 1974. Biographical sketch, brief critical study, Leskov's language.

DRUGOV, BORIS. *N. S. Leskov: ocherk tvorchestvo.* Moscow, 1961. Brief and fairly orthodox introduction to Leskov.

EDGERTON, WILLIAM B. "Leskov and Tolstoy: Two Literary Heretics." *The American Slavic and East European Review,* 12, No. 4 (1953), 524–34. By no means exhaustive, but clarifies Leskov's views on nonviolence.

_____. "Nikolai Leskov: The Intellectual Developments of a Literary Nonconformist." Diss. Columbia, 1954. Intellectual biography to 1875; some valuable biographical data and critical insights.

EEKMAN, THOMAS A. "The Genesis of Leskov's *Soborjane.*" *California Slavic Studies,* 2 (1963), 121–40. The origins of *Cathedral Folk* and a critical evaluation.

EIKHENBAUM, BORIS. "Leskov i sovremennaia proza." *Literatura. Teoriia. Kritika. Polemika.* Leningrad, 1927, pp. 210–25. Leskov as a pioneer of *skaz* and ornamental prose.

_____. " 'Chrezmernyi' pisatel' (k 100-letiiu rozhdeniia N. Leskova)." *O proze: sbornik statei.* Leningrad, 1969, pp. 327–45. An early attempt to "rehabilitate" Leskov. Focuses on style.

FARESOV, A. I. *Protiv techenii. N. S. Leskov, ego zhizn', sochineniia, polemika i vospominaniia o nem.* St. Petersburg, 1904. Not always reliable, yet contains much biographical material and personal glimpses unavailable elsewhere.

GEBEL', VALENTINA. *N. S. Leskov v tvorcheskoi laboratorii.* Moscow, 1945. Useful information on archive material and on Leskov's approach to his craft.

GIRKE, WOLFGANG. *Studien zur Sprache N. S. Leskovs. Slavistische Beiträge,* 39. Munich: Otto Sagner, 1969. Analysis of the diverse elements of Leskov's literary language.

GROSSMAN, LEONID. *N. S. Leskov: zhizn' — tvorchestvo — poetika.* Moscow, 1945. A most valuable critical-biographical study.

LESKOV, ANDREI. *N. S. Leskov. Po ego lichnym, semeinym i nesemeinym zapisiam i pamiatiam.* Moscow, 1954. Its jumble contains a wealth of information. The single most important biographical source.

MCLEAN, HUGH. "Ivan, Dough and a Kolyvan' Husband: Leskov Confronts the Germans." *Mnemozina: studia litteraria russica in honorem Vsevolod Setchkarev.* Ed. Joachim T. Baer and Norman Ingham.

Munich: Wilhelm Fink Verlag, 1974, pp. 267–80. Fine studies of "A Will of Iron" and "A Kolyvan' Husband."

————. "Leskov and Ioann of Kronstadt: On the Origins of Polunoscniki." *The American Slavic and East European Review,* 12, No. 1 (1953), 93–108. Background information and critical evaluation of "Nightowls."

————. *Nikolai Leskov: The Man and His Art.* Cambridge, Mass.: Harvard Univ. Press, 1977. Published after this study was written, the most comprehensive critical-biographical study of Leskov in any language.

PLESHCHUNOV, N. S. *Romany Leskova "Nekuda" i "Soboriane."* Baku, 1963. No critical insights but some useful information about the writing and publication of *No Way Out* and *Cathedral Folk.*

PRITCHETT, V. S. "A Russian Outsider." *The Living Novel and Later Appreciations.* New York: Random House, 1964, pp. 420–26. A general appreciation of Leskov.

SETSCHKAREFF, V. *N. S. Leskov: Sein Leben und sein Werk.* Wiesbaden: Otto Harrassowitz, 1959. Compact but thorough study of Leskov's writings; biographical sketch. Very useful.

TROITSKII, V. IU. *Leskov-khudozhnik.* Moscow, 1974. Leskov's approach to his art. Uneven, but not without interest.

VOLYNSKII, A. L. (A. L. FLEKSER). *N. S. Leskov: kriticheskii ocherk.* St. Petersburg, 1898. The first extensive critical study of Leskov. Some interesting ideas, but too heavily weighted toward religious aspects of Leskov's writings.

ZELINSKY, BODO. *Roman und Romanchronik: Strukturuntersuchungen zur Erzählkunst Nikolaj Leskovs.* Cologne and Vienna, 1970. Very pedantic and detailed structural studies of *No Way Out, The Islanders, Childhood Years, A Family in Decline,* and *Cathedral Folk.*

Index

163